LOCKE
BERKELEY
HUME

BY

C. R. MORRIS

Fellow, Tutor, and
Jowett Lecturer in Philosophy
Balliol College, Oxford

OXFORD UNIVERSITY PRESS

Oxford University Press, Amen House, London E.C. 4

GLASGOW NEW YORK TORONTO MELBOURNE WELLINGTON
BOMBAY CALCUTTA MADRAS KARACHI LAHORE DACCA
CAPE TOWN SALISBURY NAIROBI IBADAN ACCRA
KUALA LUMPUR HONG KONG

FIRST EDITION 1931
Reprinted lithographically in Great Britain
by LOWE & BRYDONE (PRINTERS) LTD., LONDON
from sheets of the first edition
1937, 1946, 1949, 1952, 1959, 1963

PREFACE

IN the section on Locke, I am chiefly indebted to Professor J. Gibson's book, *Locke's Theory of Knowledge*, which has always seemed to me to be all that such a book should be. As will be readily seen, I have used freely Mr. G. A. Johnstone's *The Development of Berkeley's Philosophy*, especially in connexion with Berkeley's moral theory and the later development of his views concerning the nature of universals. In the course of my work on Hume, I have received most stimulus from M. E. Halévy's short but brilliant references to him in his *Growth of Philosophical Radicalism*.

I wish to express my thanks to the Provost of Oriel for his kindness in reading the manuscript and making numerous suggestions, which have been gratefully adopted; to the Master of Balliol for many suggestions and for constant help and encouragement; and also to Mr. O. de Selincourt and to my wife, who kindly read the proofs.

My last and deepest acknowledgement is to Professor H. A. Prichard, to whose teaching alone I owe all my interest in philosophy.

OXFORD,   C. R. M.
November 1930.

CONTENTS

INTRODUCTION

IN treating of Locke, Berkeley, and Hume, we are dealing with what has been commonly regarded as the greatest age of British philosophy. In medieval times there had been a long line of thinkers of British birth, from John the Scot to William of Ockham, who earned an honourable place in the history of philosophy; but it may be said that their nationality was accidental and irrelevant to their thought. They wrote in Latin, and shared in and contributed to that international community of culture which went with the Latin language. After the Renaissance and before the time of Locke came the great systems of Bacon and of Hobbes, not to mention a number of lesser thinkers; and in the work of these not only original thinking, but also some distinctively English features may be traced. But their philosophies were flashes in the pan, however brilliant; they founded no great school, and, in so far as they had any general influence at all, they rather stimulated their contemporaries and followers to criticism than inspired them to follow in their tradition.

Similarly after the time of Locke, Berkeley, and Hume there came a period of stagnation, almost of death, to speculative philosophy in Britain. It was almost as if these philosophers had with rapid strides carried their great idea so far ahead of the real comprehension of their generation that time was needed before a new step forward could be taken. For forty years after the publication of Hume's *Treatise*, no philosophical work of first-class importance was published to take up his challenge; and when the new movement did begin the centre of philosophical interest moved to Germany. In Britain the ideas of Hume were being developed and applied in the special fields of politics and of psychology, while some of the greatest British thinkers were engaged in developing the classical theory of the new science of Economics. In general philosophy, J. S. Mill, it is true, did much to systematize and consolidate the work of his predecessors; indeed he gave to the logic of empiricism its classical statement. But philosophy never really came to life again in Britain until the late Victorian age, when the thought of Kant and Hegel had been already assimilated and criticized, and there arose and flowered the school of British Idealists, with F. H. Bradley as its most brilliant figure. Even that illustrious age, however, can hardly pretend to wrest the palm from that of Locke, Berkeley, and Hume.

It is well known that in the seventeenth century there began a great era in modern philosophy. It was inevitable that men should begin the attempt to square their beliefs about God and the universe with the new theories of science. This attempt branched along two main lines; and there arose the great school of Rationalism on the continent of Europe, and that of Empiricism in Britain. On the whole, it seems to be the agreed verdict of the history of philosophy that both lines of thought were in themselves abortive. Both were gathered up in the philosophy of Kant. But, as a glance at the subsequent development of thought will show, it is possible, and perhaps inevitable, in learning the lessons of Kant, to interpret his teaching and to criticize it from the standpoint of a general position which may be either predominantly rationalist or predominantly empiricist. Modern criticism has shown that neither Kant himself, nor any of the subsequent thinkers who have learned from him, have found it possible, even if it is desirable, to adopt consistently a genuinely critical position which inclines neither to the one side nor to the other.

While, thanks to Kant, the terminology has changed, and much has been done to blunt the sharpness of the conflict and to avoid argument at cross-purposes, the main issue remains to-day, as it was in the seventeenth and eighteenth centuries, the issue between the philosophy of pure reason and the philosophy of experience.

It has sometimes been maintained that it is the chief virtue of the British empiricists, as of the great British moralists, that they were working out a common-sense point of view. Locke in particular has been acclaimed as the great common-sense philosopher, who, having neither the virtues nor the vices of the system-builder or the doctrinaire, has appealed straight to the heart of the plain man, because he shares both his general equipment and his beliefs, and also his mellow, ultimately anti-rationalist, matter-of-fact temper. In general there has seemed to be an essentially English good sense about a view which assimilates the mental processes of a Newton or an Einstein to those of a village matron reflecting on some petty remedy for the ailments of her Lucy;—and which proceeds, moreover, to work out a definitive theory of the former by reflecting on the latter. But neither this aspect of the empiricists, true and interesting as it is, nor the ease of understanding, which the clearness of their writing has caused to be inseparably associated with their philosophies, must be allowed to conceal from us the fact that behind this unpretentious and homely modesty there lies a bold and vigorous attempt to build a strikingly original theory of knowledge. In the history of philosophy this striking originality shines forth with little or nothing to dim its lustre. The Critical aim in philosophy, which reasonably seeks to scrutinize the intellectual powers of man before venturing into the rarer air of systematic metaphysics—

a method, the necessity of which in philosophy was finally vindicated by Kant—was born with the British empiricists. Theirs was the first systematic attempt to comprehend the working of the mind of man, and to define thereby what kind and extent of knowledge may be expected of the human mind. Moreover, though in their attempt at a constructive philosophy they may seem to have found a blind alley, yet the history of thought has shown that their essential hypothesis neither has been nor can be entirely rejected; like the successive hypotheses of science it needs to be transcended and included in a broader view.

Though this is not the place to argue the matter in detail, a word should perhaps be said of Locke's claim to originality. To Bacon must be given the credit that he was, to some extent inadvertently, the chief pioneer in making the English language the vehicle of philosophical thought. Furthermore, taking, as he himself said, all knowledge to be his province, he was concerned, like Locke, not so much with the advancing of any particular science as with general problems of method. His classification and criticism of the main kinds and sources of error remains a valuable and brilliant contribution to mental science; and when this inquiry led him, as it naturally did, to the attempt to explain the 'just and methodical process' of the interpretation of nature, he rightly lays great stress on the necessity of an objective scientific attitude and on the need for systematic experiment. For his influential and timely exposition of this point of view, which was not altogether original, Bacon has universally received due credit. It has been said that 'he did more than any one else to help to free the intellect from preconceived notions and to direct it to the unbiased study of facts'.[1] But we may conclude

[1] Sorley, *History of English Philosophy*, p. 34.

from the fact that the philosophical writings which followed his death show very little trace of his influence that Bacon had just failed squarely to raise the issue which required to be faced. His contemporary Harvey said of him that he 'wrote philosophy like a Lord Chancellor': and certainly he had little knowledge of the exact sciences, on whose proper method he was reflecting—he vigorously opposed the Copernican theory at the very time when that theory was being confirmed by Galileo and Kepler. Perhaps for this reason he was entirely without the critical temper of Locke or Kant. Difficulties were for him simply obstacles to be overcome by the systematic use of the intellect. It never occurred to him that in scientific inquiry the human mind is struggling against more than a possibility of complete failure in its assault on the secrets of nature; and that a previous inquiry is necessary into the limits of the intellectual powers of man. He never saw the problem as the grand problem of the relation of Mind to the Universe, and he thus failed to raise the question which is at the very heart of modern philosophy.

The same may be said more simply of Hobbes. In political theory Hobbes is by far the most brilliant and perhaps the greatest figure in the history of British thought. But even in this it fell rather to Locke to be, through Hume, the founder of the greatest British school of political theory. Hobbes' political teaching failed to gain adherents because the theory of human nature on which it was essentially based appealed neither to his own nor to any succeeding generation. It was essentially the theory of a dogmatic mechanist. It is true that he had learned, or thought he had learned, what he knew of human nature from experience, rather than from revelation or any *a priori* reasoning: and to this extent he was an empiricist.

But he was of those who never doubt that experience can teach, once and for all, lessons to which all future experience will certainly conform. He never raised the wider question of the power of experience to teach or the power of the human intellect to learn. Though he argued simply from the observation of himself and his fellows, he was fundamentally a dogmatic teacher; it is doubtful whether any man has ever felt more certain that he was right.

Of Descartes it may be said that without ever fairly raising the essential question which is faced by Locke and Kant, he threw as much light on the answer to it as any thinker. He recognized that we cannot prove to ourselves that the senses have ever given, or can ever give, certain knowledge; he recognized too that the one reliable instrument of human thought—mathematical reasoning—can never prove to us the existence of an external world. Yet he never seems to have been able to raise in himself a real doubt as to the ultimate possibility of knowledge, nor to treat questions as to our capacity to know as vital questions. He took these things for granted, and is thus rightly treated by Kant as a dogmatist. This was no doubt partly because he had a first-hand knowledge of the astonishing achievements of mathematics and physics, which inspired in him complete confidence in ultimate universal success. In any case, he never did attain the critical temper; and the passages where he endeavours to make himself face ultimate questions, as for instance in his attempted proof of the *existence* of an external world, are the weakest and least acute parts of his writings. Yet when later philosophers came, with the added interest given by their critical aim, to scrutinize the intellectual powers of man, they consented to accord to Descartes pride of place in the beginnings of modern philosophy. They found that his testimony was perhaps the more valuable for the fact that it was the first-hand evidence of a mathematician and a physicist, given unawares. Descartes urged, for instance, that though the senses cannot be trusted, yet every perception must contain in it *some* truth; and again, that though the demonstrations of mathematics produce certain knowledge, yet we can never prove by this method the *existence* even of the objects of speculative geometry. When he said these things he was not in intention answering the critical questions of Locke or of Kant; he was simply conducting his analysis honestly and exhaustively, and recording all his results. Thus, though he did not put Locke's question, he gave one answer to it—the answer of a confident believer in mathematical physics—and founded a school of Rationalists. It remained for Locke to suggest another answer, the answer of the philosophy of experience. But it is perhaps Locke's chief glory that he first put the right question, and gave to modern philosophy its true orientation.

We must not, however, allow the preoccupation with the school of empiricism or with the historical development of modern thought in general to obscure from us the philosophical greatness as individuals of Locke, Berkeley, and Hume. Like Descartes, Locke is much more than the founder of a school: like Spinoza and Leibniz, Berkeley and Hume are much more than links in a chain. Each one had a fully rounded philosophy of his own; and it would only be possible to represent them as links in a chain of thought at the cost of omitting to consider, or at least failing duly to emphasize, some of the most characteristic and most philosophically important features of their respective theories. The essentially critical attitude of Locke, the confident idealism of Berkeley, and the rationalistic naturalism of Hume must all be glossed over if the continuity in development of thought within the school is to be duly stressed. This would be to extract the very nerve of their thought, and, what is more important, to fail to explain how each of them really believed in his own philosophy.

At any rate the chief aim of this study will be, not to give in due order and proportion the history of a school—the flowering and death of a single idea through the thought of a series of writers—but rather to take each of the three in his single character as an individual thinker, and while not obscuring the relation of one to another, to attempt to give some account of the unity and balance of the views of each one, taking his philosophy as a whole. In this way it will be seen that each in his own way, by his own active genius and individual character, vindicates his own right to take his place as one of the world's great philosophers, owing little or nothing in this regard to the mere accident that in history he happened to succeed some one great thinker or to precede another. The school of empiricism, which they founded, remained to offer contributions of importance to philosophy, psychology, and politics long after their time, but there never again towered out of the chain of its history any great figure comparable to them.

LOCKE

1. *Life*

JOHN LOCKE was born on 29 August 1632 at Wrington, in Somerset, at the house of his mother's brother. His father, John Locke, was a country attorney of Puritan ancestry who lived in a small mansion, called Beluton, near the little market town of Pensford, six miles south of Bristol. Locke always speaks of his father with respect and affection, and commends him for treating him in his childhood with a severity which he gradually relaxed as time went on, until a close friendship developed between father and son. For fourteen years Locke stayed at home and was schooled by his father; this was probably in part due to the disturbed state of Bristol owing to the outbreak of the Civil War in 1642. In 1646 he was admitted to Westminster School, where he remained six years. In 1652 he was elected to a junior studentship at Christ Church in Oxford, which college he made his home for thirty years, until in 1684 he was expelled by the express order of Charles II.

Locke gained little or no satisfaction from his Oxford studies, being impatient with the 'verbal exercises' of the scholastic philosophers, which Puritan control of the University had not abolished. He thought little of his tutors, and was so discouraged that he does not seem to have been a hard-working student, but spent most of his time in reading romances. He seems to have thought at one time of entering the Church, and was offered prospects of advancement should he do so. But he preferred to take up medicine, and spent his time in medical experiments, and to some extent in amateur practice. At this time the interest of all men was turning towards experimental science. In 1660 the Royal Society had been founded in

Oxford, and was 'destined to be the chief agent in a long
series of glorious and salutary reforms'.[1] The age of faith
was passing; and Locke was to be one of the chief spokes-
men of the new questioning spirit. While his chief interest
lay in medicine, Locke gave some attention during these
years to meteorology, and some barometric records made
by him are quoted in Boyle's *History of the Air*. It is
evident from his commonplace books that he was also at
this time much interested in religious and moral questions
and in practical problems of government. His writings
already showed the fervid enthusiasm for religious toleration which remained with him all his life, and he seems
already to have formed his general theory of morality as
fundamentally based on the pursuit of happiness and the
avoidance of misery.

In 1665 Locke was drawn away from Oxford on diplo-
matic service; he acted for some months as secretary to
Sir Walter Vane, Ambassador to the Elector of Branden-
burg. In 1666 occurred the chance meeting with Lord
Ashley, afterwards first Earl of Shaftesbury, which
resulted in a lifelong friendship between the two men and
caused Locke finally to be drawn into practical political
affairs. He became medical adviser and confidential agent
to Lord Ashley and tutor to his son; he took up his
residence at Exeter House in the Strand, and remained in
the closest association with Ashley for the next fifteen
years. Here he met Sydenham, the great London physi-
cian, formed a close friendship with him, and used to go to
watch his remarkable cases. In November 1668 he was
made a Fellow of the Royal Society, though he does not
seem ever to have taken a very active part in its proceedings.
In the winter of 1670–1 at a meeting of a few friends, pro-

[1] A. C. Fraser, *Locke*, p. 18.

bably in Oxford, there was laid the foundation of Locke's life work in philosophy. While discussing some indifferent subject, the friends found that they could get no farther with their difficulties until an investigation had first been made into 'our own abilities', to see 'what objects our understandings were or were not fitted to deal with'.[1] This work Locke regarded himself as commissioned to undertake, and he spent the next twenty years, with some intervals, in the attempt to accomplish it.

Early in 1672, when Lord Ashley became President of the Board of Trade and then Lord Chancellor of England, Locke was brought into closer touch with practical affairs; he became Ashley's secretary for the presentation of benefices, and in the following year Secretary to the Board of Trade. This post he filled with diligence in spite of troublesome health until, in 1675, Shaftesbury ceased to be Chancellor. Then, acting on medical advice, he went into retirement in France for three years, which he spent partly in Paris and partly at Montpellier. While in Paris he chiefly associated, not with philosophers—he never seems to have met Malebranche, Arnauld, Spinoza, or Leibniz—but with representatives of natural science and of medicine. In 1679 he returned to London, and was at Shaftesbury's right hand through the political crisis in connexion with the succession to the throne, when Parliament attempted to exclude the Duke of York as being a Papist. After Shaftesbury's escape to Holland and subsequent death there in 1683, Locke was looked upon with suspicion. With his customary prudence he retired voluntarily to Holland. While in exile there he was by the order of Charles II deprived of his studentship at Christ Church. After the execution of Monmouth in 1685 Locke, who was

[1] *Essay*, Epistle to the Reader (p. 4).

still in Holland, was forced to go into hiding for a time, since he was regarded as a dangerous person and suspected of having been concerned in the Rebellion. At the end of 1685 the danger passed, and he was able to travel about freely in Holland and resume his association with Limborch and Le Clerc and other liberal theologians in that country.

In February 1689, after the Revolution, he returned to England. Two winters in London aggravated his chronic ailments; but at last he found rest in his retirement to Oates in Essex, a country seat of Sir Francis Masham. Lady Masham, the second wife of Sir Francis, was a daughter of Ralph Cudworth, the Anglican theological philosopher, with whose family Locke had enjoyed intimate friendship for some time before his retirement to Holland. Lady Masham now prevailed on Locke to make his permanent home at Oates 'on his own terms', and there he settled to enjoy a quiet country retirement. Esther Masham, the young daughter of Sir Francis by his first wife, became Locke's favourite companion, and we have a sprightly account of the life at Oates in their correspondence.

It was characteristic of Locke's cautious nature and methodical prudence that he published nothing in his early life. A few minor papers were contributed by him to the Bibliothèque Universelle in 1686–8, but nothing of first-rate importance was published until the *Two Treatises on Government* in 1690. The *Essay concerning Human Understanding* was apparently finished by 1679, but Locke 'thought too well of it to let it then go out of his hands', and it was not published until 1690, in the same year as the *Two Treatises*, when its author was fifty-eight years of age. This tardiness in publishing agrees with the prudent and cautious temper and the outstanding common

sense which belonged to Locke's character; it is in marked
contrast to the eager impetuosity which hurried both
Berkeley and Hume to produce their bolder and more confident speculations while they were still young men.
Throughout his life Locke's modesty kept him in the back-
ground, and it was only after long and intimate acquaintance that his friends discovered the worth of his character
and the liveliness of his mind.

In 1696 Locke accepted office as a Commissioner of
Trade, and notwithstanding his bad health he was the
most efficient and among the most regular of the commis-
sioners. More than once he asked leave to resign, until at
last in 1700 the king accepted his resignation. Locke then
settled into complete retirement at Oates, and began
methodically to set his affairs in order in expectation of the
end. In the spring of 1704 he began to decline; he was
nursed through the summer by Esther and Lady Masham,
and on 28 October of that year he died.

2. *Theory of Knowledge.*

Locke's avowed purpose in writing the *Essay concerning
Human Understanding* was 'to enquire into the original,
certainty, and extent of human Knowledge, together with
the grounds and degrees of Belief, Opinion, and Assent.'[1]
He had no wish to concern himself with difficulties regarding either the general nature of mind or the special mechanism of perception; indeed he always regarded the inter-
relations of mind and body as presenting such insuperable difficulty as not even to be a proper object of investigation. His intention was a modest one; he proposed to
adopt what he called an 'historical, plain method'[2] of
inquiry, and he hoped in this way to be able to give some

[1] *Essay*, I. i. 2.   [2] Ibid.

account of the ways in which our understandings come to have such knowledge as we possess, and thus to determine the 'measures of the certainty of our knowledge, or the grounds of those persuasions which are to be found amongst men, so various, different, and wholly contradictory'.[1] In other words Locke proposed, taking for granted the existence among mankind of knowledge concerning some things and of opinion regarding others, to search out the distinction between opinion and knowledge, and to examine 'by what measures, in things whereof we have no certain knowledge, we ought to regulate our assent, and moderate our persuasions'.[2] He realized that there is considerable risk that men will overestimate the certainty which attaches to some of their beliefs, and perhaps that there was some small danger that they would underestimate the certainty of others; and it was his aim to remove such errors once and for all.

Thus Locke was in a sense more philosophical in outlook than his predecessors. Bacon and Hobbes had both taken for granted the competence and validity of scientific reasoning to produce certain knowledge, and had confined their inquiry to an analysis of its method of working. Even Descartes seems to have assumed without criticism that there is no problem which reason cannot solve if used according to a correct 'method', and no object the nature of which it can not fully comprehend. These sweeping claims on behalf of science Locke is not prepared to accept. He recognizes that human knowledge is likely to have its limits, and he thinks it is the business of philosophy to determine those limits. It is indeed easy to see how, coming after Locke, Hume was induced to raise the more fundamental question whether knowledge was possible

[1] *Essay*, I. i. 2.　　　　[2] Ibid. 3.

at all, though Locke himself is far from occupying this extreme position. Rather he takes up the standpoint of common sense; he assumes that knowledge is possible, and that a good deal of knowledge has in fact been achieved, but he sees no good reason for insisting that belief or opinion must be either developed into knowledge or repudiated as illusion. He accepts both knowledge and belief as plainly existing in rational beings, and simply wishes to distinguish between them, to determine their proper spheres, and to discover the grounds on which each is based.

Locke's position is therefore quite clear. It is not his aim (as it was the aim of Descartes) to discover what is the true method of reason, in order to be enabled to use this method for the solution of fresh problems in natural philosophy. He wishes rather to clear the ground by determining the proper limits to the use of reason; to defend its use perhaps at one point where it is commonly attacked for being presumptuous, to repudiate its claims at another point where it too easily thinks to have proved its thesis. The actual work of advancing human knowledge he modestly leaves to others. 'The commonwealth of learning', he says, 'is not at this time without master-builders, whose mighty designs in advancing the sciences will leave lasting monuments to the admiration of posterity; but every one must not hope to be a Boyle or a Sydenham; and in an age that produces such masters as the great Huygenius, and the incomparable Mr. Newton, with some other of that strain, it is ambition enough to be employed as an under-labourer in clearing the ground a little, and removing some of the rubbish that lies in the way to knowledge.' [1]

[1] *Essay*, Epistle to the Reader, *ad fin*.

Locke's first task was therefore a negative one, since there was, as he saw, much rubbish to be cleared away. In his youth at Oxford he had suffered much from the 'depraved Aristotelianism' of the day. In the doctrine of the schools all reasoning was regarded as a process of subsumption; new knowledge of nature was thought to be arrived at by drawing hitherto unrecognized conclusions from a comparatively small number of general principles, these principles themselves being beyond question and claiming exemption from the bar of critical reason on the plea of being innate. The discoveries of science were thus only acceptable if they could be represented as implied by the accepted first principles; if they could not be shown to be thus implied, the current philosophy required that they should be repudiated, however strong might be the empirical and experimental evidence for accepting them. Locke saw that these syllogistic tests based on supposedly self-evident truths were mere 'rubbish in the way to knowledge', and he felt that the time had come to join issue fundamentally with the philosophy which supported and justified them. He regarded it as an urgent task of first-rate importance to destroy once and for all the appeal to innate origin as a guarantee of the truth of any general principle or law. Evidently this crude doctrine that the first principles of knowledge are innate in every human being could claim very general credence in Locke's day, since it provoked from him a lengthy and careful attack. This part of his work seems merely tedious at the present day; and it is difficult now to think that there was ever here a live issue, or that any thinker of repute ever differed from Locke on this point.[1]

[1] Certainly the view which Locke is attacking was not Aristotle's own view; nor can it fairly be attributed to Descartes or Leibniz.

It must not be thought that Locke's attack on innate principles marks him as in any way a sceptic. He is not, in intention at least, denying the certainty of the principles in question; he is arguing that their certainty (on which he lays emphasis) is not due to their being innate. When we accept a principle as certain we do not do so because it is innate, he urges, but because the consideration of the nature of the things represented by the terms of the principle will not suffer us to think otherwise, how or whensoever we are brought to reflect on them. Further, his lack of any scepticism is shown by his accepting without hesitation the implied challenge to give the correct explanation of the origin of knowledge of these principles—an explanation compatible with the obvious fact that when a scientist, or indeed any one, comes to criticize the validity of a first principle and so to examine its origin, he does not set himself to investigate the mental equipment of primitive savages or of new-born babes in order to determine whether this particular law is among the innate principles of which they are aware at the dawn of intelligence, but rather applies himself to observe and examine the real things of whose nature the principle is said to be a principle. In this Locke seems to be emphasizing the common-sense claim that in the end our knowledge of the world around us must come from an examination of the world around us, and not from an introspective analysis of the furniture of our minds. In thus setting out to explain how all our knowledge arises from perceptual experience he thinks he is simply setting down in plain language an account of the method which the scientist does in fact pursue; and he expects to be able without much difficulty to show how by perceptual experience alone we can come to certain knowledge—for instance, knowledge of the mathematical axioms. This, however, was a task which, as we shall see, proved to be beyond his powers.

It is not necessary to enter in detail into Locke's destructive criticism of the doctrine of innate ideas. It was easy for him to show that most of the principles which were supposed to be innate are so general and abstruse as to appear meaningless except to those who are already disciplined in mind. These laws, so far from being innate and present in the mind at birth, are in fact the fruit of long experience and training. They are not even universally consented to; nor, if they were, would this prove them to be true. In fact, Locke easily shows that if we are in doubt of the truth of a principle, to inquire whether or not it be innate is wasted labour.

Locke now finds himself bound to give some constructive account of the way in which the first principles of knowledge are apprehended. Since man is born with no knowledge innate in him, his mind at birth must be, according to Locke, a kind of 'tabula rasa', ready to receive impressions, but not yet having received any.[1] All the knowledge, then, and all the beliefs which have been acquired by man in the course of the ages, must be shown to be wholly and completely founded on the experiences of individual men during their lives. All the ideas which are in the mind must have been come by, Locke maintains, through human experience between birth and death. Thus he is committed to produce a complete systematic theory of knowledge based upon a common-sense principle which everybody believes; namely that knowledge is derived from an examination of the objects of which the knowledge is knowledge, and not from any other source whatever. Locke's attempt is of vital interest because of

[1] Cf. *Essay*, II. i. 2.

the common-sense and obviously sound nature of the
view he seeks to maintain; and the unprejudiced reader
will probably approach the matter, as Locke approached it,
anticipating little difficulty in bringing the main part of the
inquiry to a successful conclusion.

From this point Locke's inquiry becomes psychological,
in the sense that he tries by analysing actual mental processes to discover in what way we do in fact, in conscious
experience, arrive at the beliefs which we hold; his hope
being that he will then be able to determine the validity of
beliefs arrived at in this way. It is to be noticed that he
assumed, as all his followers previous to J. S. Mill assumed
after him, that the validity of a belief depends upon the
way in which we arrive at it; the method of proof was
assumed to be the same as the method of discovery. He
seeks to discover how we normally come to apprehend
such principles as we believe to be true, and he assumes
that this discovery will in itself enable him to determine
whether or not those principles are true. The truth is that
it does not follow, because men have believed a thing for
inadequate reasons or for a wrong reason, that therefore
their belief is false; it does not even follow, because men
have hitherto been unable to prove a particular principle
or have put their faith in spurious proofs, that therefore
it cannot be proved. Thus it would seem that Locke was
wrong in assuming that as he came to discover how men
do in fact come to their beliefs, he would by the same
inquiry be determining whether or not those beliefs were
true. As Kant saw, Locke's psychological method was not
in itself competent to achieve his critical aim.

. It may also be pointed out that Locke was clearly wrong
in thinking that his rejection of innate knowledge as a basis
for belief in itself forced him to regard the mind as a 'tabula

rasa.' It would have been equally compatible with this general position to put forward the Kantian hypothesis that the mind is capable of activity in cognitive experience; that is, that instead of being a mere 'tabula rasa' ready and waiting to receive impressions, the mind is gifted, as part of its essential nature, with capacities to do something to or make something of any impressions which it receives, though these capacities can of course only manifest themselves by operation when they are given impressions to act upon—that is, in the course of sentient experience. There is nothing in Locke's attack on innate principles which could fairly be taken to exclude this view. Yet Locke never explicitly puts it forward; though, as we shall see, much of his teaching, in distinction from that of his follower Hume, really implies it. Why then did he not frankly adopt this view instead of the 'tabula rasa' doctrine? The answer seems to be that Locke, like all the pre-Kantians, condemned the view out of hand in so far as they straitly considered it, and always sought, if unsuccessfully, to avoid any doctrine which showed any tendency toward such a view, because of the right and proper instinct that this hypothesis must always represent knowing as making or constructing, instead of recognizing its true character as not creation, but discovery or apprehension. If in knowledge the mind is active and does something to the impressions it receives, then, in the end, it makes or alters; and making or altering is incompatible with knowing. For this excellent reason, Locke insisted, almost without realizing it, on the passivity of the mind, and attempted to represent knowledge as wholly dependent on impressions received. This is to say that he rejected the view that the mind is active as being evidently inadmissible; so evidently indeed that no proof need be given. It was not until after the failure of Locke's hypothesis that it seemed reasonable even to canvass Kant's difficult and paradoxical view.

Be this as it may, Locke now confessedly sets out to discover in what way we do in fact arrive at knowledge. Every man, he says, is conscious to himself that he thinks;[1] and that which his mind is applied about whilst thinking being the ideas which are there, it is past doubt that men have in their minds several ideas. Since these ideas are none of them innate, how do our minds come to be filled with ideas? If we examine all the ideas that we have, he says, we find that they all come from two sources—sensation and reflection. It is not difficult to find instances of ideas of reflection; such are the ideas of perceiving, thinking, doubting, believing, reasoning, willing—and in general the ideas of all such things as are not sensible are ideas of reflection. Ideas of sensation provide more difficulty, since they must 'depend wholly upon our senses',[2] and must presumably arise independently of any reflection. To us it might appear that the mind cannot receive anything which can fairly be called an idea without some reflection. It is necessary, therefore, in view of this consideration, to attend carefully to the instances of ideas of sensation given by Locke himself. 'Our senses', he says, 'conversant about particular sensible objects, do convey into the mind several distinct perceptions of things according to those various ways wherein those objects do affect them; and thus we come by those *ideas* we have of yellow, white, heat, cold, soft, hard, bitter, sweet, and all those which we call sensible qualities.'[3] It is difficult to see how any ideas of heat or cold could be arrived at without some reflection; these ideas seem to be dependent upon the

[1] See *Essay*, II. i. I. [2] Ibid., 3. [3] Ibid.

activities of comparison and abstraction, so that in the reception of them the mind cannot rightly be regarded as merely receiving sensations.

Locke's purpose, however, in making this distinction is clear. He sees that when we think we think *about* something, and that without something to think about we cannot think; therefore that which we think about must be provided by some means other than thinking. Since he cannot admit 'innate principles' from which thinking may start, their place is supplied on his view by these 'simple ideas of sensation' about which thought occupies itself, but which do not at all depend for their own existence upon the activity of thought. The mind must be provided with ideas before it can think, and these ideas, since they do not come from thinking, must necessarily come into the mind through the senses. If then prior to thought ideas must come into the mind through the senses, we should be able by an analysis of perceptual experience to detect their passage into the mind and so to determine their nature. This is what Locke is trying to do, somewhat confusedly, in his account of simple ideas of sensation. He notices that there are simple qualities of objects which we apprehend immediately and not by thinking, as for instance that a poker is hot or that a rose is red. This fact he expresses by saying that the idea of the heat of the poker or the idea of the redness of the rose comes into the mind by sensation. When he generalizes from this that the ideas of heat and cold, or of white and red, are simple ideas of sensation, he is in difficulties; for clearly the idea of heat has no meaning except in so far as heat is distinguished from cold, and this distinction cannot be made without thinking. Whatever it is then which is 'given' to the mind in sensation, it is not, for instance, the 'idea of heat'; and so far, therefore, Locke has failed to discover what are those simple ideas of sensation with which reflection occupies itself.

This unsatisfactory result is in part due to the fact that Locke's method in this part of his argument is not as empirical and psychological as it should have been, or as he intended it to be. Having convinced himself that the ideas with which thought deals arise in the mind in sense-perception, he should have applied himself to a careful unprejudiced analysis of sense-perception in order to discover exactly what we are aware of in perceiving, always being careful to distinguish that of which we are immediately aware from that which we conclude from our immediate awareness. Now admittedly this is a difficult task requiring special discipline; but it is hard to believe that any one who had honestly attempted it could have thereby come to the view that in perception we are aware of a series of ideas of simple qualities following one another in the mind. When we look at a house, for instance, for a period of time, it is perhaps plausible to argue that we are aware of it part by part, the ideas of the various parts succeeding one another in the mind as we shift our gaze; but it is hardly plausible to say we are aware of it quality by quality in this way. Yet this is Locke's official account of the nature of perception.

The truth is clearly that Locke's view was not arrived at by such an analysis of perception at all. Rather, seeing that we think in terms of simple qualities, he concluded that simple qualities must be given in sensation, and spent little time or effort in attempting to determine whether psychological investigation of sensation confirmed this view. In order to think, we must be provided with ideas like heat and cold, colour, softness, and bitterness; therefore since these ideas are not innate, and, as being the materials of thought, are not generated by thought itself, they *must* be given in sensation. Whence else could they come? The argument is plausible enough, but it is hardly a proper argument for an empirical inquirer. In emphasizing that sense-perception plays an essential part in knowledge, and that it has a function to fulfil which can never be fulfilled by thought, Locke offered an important contribution to theory of knowledge, and insisted on a point which the Cartesians failed to notice. But he should have regarded this doctrine as being a challenge to him to demonstrate the importance of sense-perception by a fair-minded scientific exposition of its nature; instead of which he regarded himself as provided at one blow with an obviously correct theory of perception without the need of any proper analysis, and thus was led to found a professedly empirical philosophy on an unrecognized and uncriticized dogma.[1]

It is important, however, to understand just what was Locke's theory of perception. As we have already seen, he thought of the mind as being purely passive in the reception of ideas of sensation; the object in a sense 'imprints' itself upon the mind. 'These simple ideas, when offered to the mind, the understanding can no more refuse to have, nor alter when they are imprinted, nor blot them out and make new ones itself, than a mirror can refuse, alter or obliterate the images or ideas, which the objects set before it do therein produce.'[2] According to Locke the nature of the ideas arriving in our minds through the senses is entirely determined by the nature of the objects, and not

---

[1] As we shall see, Locke's theory of perception had serious and far-reaching consequences in the thought of Berkeley and Hume, who never fully recognized its spurious nature.

[2] *Essay*, II. i. 25.

at all by the nature of the mind, just as the nature of the images in a mirror, he says, is wholly determined by the nature of the objects set before the mirror. In point of fact such images are to some extent affected by the nature of the particular mirror, and there is a clear sense in which a mirror can 'distort' images. This point Locke does not consider; all that he actually says, however, is true—that the image cannot be altered by the mirror when once it is imprinted. But his ill-grounded confidence that ideas are exactly 'like' the objects of which they are ideas seems to be in part due to this oversight.

All ideas of sensation come into the mind 'simple' according to Locke; they are never confused or complex. When we look at a thing we do not, he thinks, see a confused jumble of qualities, but we see first one quality and then another; ideas of the various qualities enter the mind in sequence, one by one. 'Though the qualities that affect our senses are, in the things themselves, so united and blended that there is no separation, no distance between them; yet it is plain the ideas they produce in the mind enter by the senses simple and unmixed.'[1] Locke does not ask himself how or why it comes about that while the qualities exist together in the object blended and unseparated, yet the ideas of the qualities enter the mind one by one; he simply asserts that they in fact do so. The ideas of sensation, he says, are unquestionably simple and distinct in the mind—'the coldness and hardness which a man feels in a piece of ice being as distinct ideas in the mind as the smell and whiteness of a lily, or as the taste of sugar and the smell of a rose; and there is nothing can be plainer to a man than the clear and distinct perception he has of those simple ideas'.[2] Here no doubt Locke is right

[1] Ibid., ii. 1.   [2] Ibid.

in pointing out that the smell of a rose and its colour are separate ideas, in the sense that no one could think them to be one idea or confuse one with the other; but it does not really follow from this that they are separate in the sense that they must enter the mind one after the other, and that we cannot ever be aware of both at one and the same moment of time.

All those ideas in our minds which are not simple are said by Locke to be compounded of simple ideas. We put together a number of ideas of simple qualities and so form the complex idea of a horse or a table. Indeed, this is the way in which all our knowledge comes into being; there can arise no knowledge from any other source. 'All those sublime thoughts which tower above the clouds, and reach as high as heaven itself, take their rise and footing here; in all that great extent wherein the mind wanders in those remote speculations it may seem to be elevated with, it stirs not one jot beyond those ideas which *sense* or *reflection* have offered for its contemplation.' [1]

Having given some account of the way in which the mind comes by all its ideas, Locke passes on to determine what is the relation between the ideas and the objects of which they are ideas.[2] In this connexion he finds it necessary to draw an important distinction. Simple ideas, he says, are of two kinds; some of them are ideas of primary qualities, and these 'resemble' qualities which in reality belong to the object; others are ideas of secondary qualities, and in these cases there are, strictly speaking, no qualities in the object which these ideas resemble. By quality here Locke means, or says that he means, the 'power which a subject has to produce an idea in the mind'. Some of these 'powers' or qualities are utterly inseparable

[1] *Essay*, II. i. 24.   [2] Ibid., viii. 7 seq.

from the body in whatever state it be; they are such that sense constantly finds them in every particle of matter which has bulk enough to be perceived, and the mind finds them inseparable from every particle of matter, even though it be so small as to be singly imperceptible by the senses. These qualities are the primary qualities—namely solidity, extension, figure, motion or rest, and number.

Other qualities there are (which Locke calls 'qualities' only in deference to common usage) which are really nothing in the objects themselves, but only powers which the objects have to produce various sensations in us by their primary qualities. These he calls secondary qualities, and he gives as instances colours, sounds, and tastes—ideas which are produced in us, he thinks, by the bulk, figure, texture, and motion of the insensible parts of objects. He classes as secondary qualities those powers also which bodies have to affect other bodies, since, he urges, the power of fire to produce a new colour or different consistency in wax or clay is as much a quality of fire as the power it has to produce in me a sensation of warmth or of burning.

Locke's view is then that the ideas of primary qualities are resemblances of real qualities; their 'patterns' do exist in the bodies themselves; whereas the ideas we have of secondary qualities bear no resemblance to the bodies, being caused in us by qualities in the bodies which they do not in the least resemble—that is, the primary qualities. We may notice that Locke is here using the word 'idea' in a quite different sense; he is no longer thinking of the simple ideas with which the mind 'occupies itself when it thinks', such as the idea of green or of yellow, of heat or of cold; rather he means the mental impression we receive of a particular thing that is green or yellow, hot or cold. It seems fair to say that he is thinking of an idea as a mental picture of the object, produced in our minds by our looking at the object. It is by receiving a number of mental pictures of this kind of the same object and then in some sense compounding them or putting them together, that, on Locke's view, we come to apprehend an object. In the case of the primary qualities the mental impressions 'resemble' real qualities in the object, presumably as a portrait resembles its original; while in the case of secondary qualities there are not, strictly speaking, any qualities in the object for the impressions to resemble. An object appears to have shape, and it really has shape; it also appears to have colour, but in reality it has no colour.

Locke is thus inviting us to draw a distinction between appearance and reality; and, this being so, it will help us to make his view clear if we attempt to determine more accurately what he thought was the true nature of reality. It may perhaps be objected that this attempt is an improper one, since we cannot apprehend reality except as it appears; if there is a reality which does not appear, in some sense underlying the appearances, we cannot know it. This difficulty however need not disturb us now, since it did not occur to Locke; and if we represent him as being more critical than in fact he was, we shall fail to understand what was in his mind. On Locke's view, then, if I set up before me a cubical block of stone, it appears white but is not really white; it appears cold but is not really cold; it appears to have shape and really has shape. In particular it appears cubical—but is it really cubical? It appears to be at rest, but is it really at rest or moving? Strange as it may seem, it is very difficult to determine what was Locke's answer to these questions. At times, when he is speaking of primary qualities, Locke seems to mean that particular things have the actual qualities which they appear to have; if they appear cubical they are cubical; if they appear at rest they are at rest; and probably as a matter of fact Locke hardly questioned this. Yet at other times he seems to be more cautious, and asserts, more in the manner of Descartes, only that it is inseparable from the nature of body that it should have some figure and that it should be either at rest or in motion. On this view he might quite consistently have admitted that we are sometimes deceived as to the actual figure a particular body has; it must have some figure, but this does not necessarily mean that in perception we immediately apprehend its true figure. But it is not possible to determine certainly what Locke's view was on this essential point.

The truth is that his distinction between primary and secondary qualities is only very incompletely worked out. Clearly his view is rather negative than positive, and arises from a criticism of the common view in the light of current scientific theories of matter. He professes to arrive at the distinction by an examination of common opinion; but the wording of this section is admittedly influenced by 'the judicious Mr. Newton's incomparable book';[1] and it is the doctrines of physics that Locke really had in mind throughout. When a body appears white, it is insensible motions of its minute parts which make it appear so; in the object there is no whiteness but only motion—a primary quality. Clearly Locke is here accepting the physicist's account of the world as a true account of reality, and wishes to show that it has saved mankind from an old error which, he thinks, uncritically confused a mere appearance with the true reality. It is on physics that the distinction between primary and secondary qualities is really based.

[1] *Essay*, II. viii. 11, note.

If Locke had fully realized this, however, and had continued his inquiry along the same lines, his view must have been very different from that at which he actually arrived. This will at once be clearly seen if we consider the problem of substance. Following on from his distinction of primary and secondary qualities as we have expounded it, we should have expected Locke to put to himself the problem of substance in this way: what is that which has the primary qualities? Extension and motion imply something to move and to be extended; when the physicist explains heat and colour in terms of motion, what is this something which moves? So the discussion of the problem of substance must inevitably have become a discussion of the nature of the 'atoms' or 'minute particles' of physics. Leibniz, who really understood physics, saw the problem in this light; and both Kant and modern philosophers have followed him. But for Locke, who based himself on common sense, the problem of substance was a quite different one. It will be wise first to summarize quite baldly Locke's official discussion of the problem of substance.

What we are aware of when we perceive, he says, is simple uncompounded ideas of primary and secondary qualities. Now we cannot imagine that the qualities of which these ideas are ideas can subsist of themselves; we therefore accustom ourselves to suppose some substratum wherein they subsist, which we call 'substance'. Yet, 'if any one will examine himself concerning his notion of pure substance in general, he will find he has no other idea of it at all, but only a supposition of he knows not what support of such qualities which are capable of producing simple ideas in us'.[1] If we are asked in what subject

[1] *Essay*, II. xxiii. 2.

colour or weight or other secondary qualities inhere, we
say the solid extended parts; if asked in what these primary
qualities of solidity and extension inhere, we reply in substance—therein talking like children, who when in a difficulty use words of which they know not the meaning.
The truth is that by making for ourselves a complex idea
of something extended, figured, and coloured, we are 'as
far from the idea of the substance of body as if we knew
nothing at all.' [1]

Thus our ideas of particular substances are clear enough
because they are simply complexes of simple ideas of
sensible qualities; but of substance in general we have no
clear idea at all. Three sorts of ideas go to make up our
complex ideas of particular substances; first, ideas of
primary qualities which do really inhere in the things;
secondly, of sensible secondary qualities, which ideas 'are
not in the things themselves otherwise than as anything is
in its cause'; [2] thirdly, 'the aptness we consider in any
substance to give or receive such alterations of primary
qualities as that the substance so altered should produce
in us different ideas from what it did before; these are
called active and passive powers: all which powers, as far
as we have any notice or notion of them, terminate only in
sensible simple ideas.' [3] True substance whether of body
or of spirit is unknown to us. It appears that God did not
intend finite beings to have a clear and perfect comprehension of it; but we have such knowledge as is suitable to our state. 'We are furnished,' in Locke's own
words, 'with faculties (dull and weak as they are) to discover enough in the creatures to lead us to the knowledge
of the Creator, and to the knowledge of our duty; and
we are fitted well enough with abilities to provide for

[1] Ibid., 16.   [2] Ibid., 9.   [3] Ibid.

the conveniences of living; these are our business in this world.'[1] But to comprehend the nature of substance is too much for our understanding.

Now it is clear that an examination of the method and conclusions of science would never have led Locke to raise the problem of substance in this form; nor would it have allowed him to rest satisfied with such an inconclusive answer. If the physicist proposes to explain everything ultimately in terms of the motion of particles, he must ultimately give some account of the nature of those particles; he cannot ultimately admit that he is speaking like a child, who in a difficulty uses words of which he knows not the meaning. He must either deny that there exists anything but motion, accepting the paradox that there is a motion without anything to move, or he must give some account of the nature of that which moves. Clearly, however, Locke is not looking at this problem, as Leibniz does, from the clear-cut point of view of a physicist. It would seem that he no longer has science primarily in mind, nor even metaphysics, but rather logic. Certainly the distinction between substance and its qualities is not for Locke a distinction between appearance and reality—since he thinks of the primary qualities themselves as real. Further, when he has science in mind he seems to regard reality as knowable, in that the man of science is assumed to discover the truth about it; substance on the other hand Locke declares to be unknowable. What then had Locke in mind in distinguishing between this so-called substance and its qualities?

At first sight it might seem tempting to conclude that Locke, for all his revolt from Aristotelianism, had allowed himself to become tied up in current philosophical jargon,

[1] *Essay*, II. xxiii. 12.

and was in the most obvious sense discussing 'something
he knew not what'; that is to say that he had become
entangled in a mere verbal discussion, so that the real problem had passed entirely out of sight, and the question
actually being discussed was on his own principles not a
real problem at all. It may at once be admitted that the
part played by the conception of substance in the current
philosophy, which Locke repudiates, would to a large
extent explain his pre-occupation with the subject. But
it would be a mistake to treat this discussion in Locke as
wholly due to a mere uncriticized survival from scholasti-
cism, as Berkeley seems to do. Starting from the point of
view of common sense, Locke seems to be facing a genuine
difficulty. He is right in arguing that we cannot think of
qualities as existing in themselves; there must be something in which they inhere. Further, we do not think of
an object as merely *being* the sum of its qualities; there
must be something over and above the qualities, which
holds the qualities together and makes the object an object;
without this something the qualities would fall apart and
not make a unity at all. Yet of this something we can
receive no idea; it cannot be apprehended by sense, since
everything that is apprehended by sense is a quality. From
this it follows, on the principles of the empirical philosophy,
that it cannot be apprehended at all. The most that we
can say is that there must be something there, though we
can know nothing about it; it is 'something we know not
what'.

If we press Locke as regards the nature of ultimate
reality, it would seem that he thought of both substance
and primary qualities as being real, and that therefore he
thought of reality as partially knowable and partially
unknowable—the primary qualities of it knowable, and the

substance of it unknowable, since God thought it unnecessary to our state that we should know substance. No doubt it is difficult to maintain this view, or even to state it consistently; nevertheless it seems to have been Locke's view. He did not feel the necessity of thinking that only that which is through and through known can be asserted to be real, and he found no difficulty in thinking of the real as in part essentially unknowable to us, nor of the partially unknowable as being real; nor did he think that its partial unknowability was any hindrance to its being partially knowable. Had he been pressed on these points it is impossible to tell what answer he would have given; for when Berkeley and Hume did emphasize these difficulties he was not there to reply. But one thing is clear; Locke took it for granted that even in the ultimate account the world would be found to consist of particular substances or 'things'; and any such doctrine has to face the problem of substance in the form in which he propounded it. Locke did not consider that the physical theories on which his distinction between primary and secondary qualities rests were incompatible with a belief in the ultimate reality of particular substances or things. Hence he thought his problem of substance a real one.

This lack of criticism on Locke's part becomes further clear if we consider his view of *relations*. The understanding, he says, in the consideration of anything, is not confined to that precise object; it can, as it were, bring one thing and set it by another, and carry its view from the one thing to the other; the things so brought together are said to be *related*. Things are capable of almost infinitely varied consideration in respect of other things; moreover the ideas of relations are often far clearer than the ideas of the substances which are related; but relations 'terminate

in and are concerned about'[1] the simple ideas either of
sensation or reflection, which Locke thinks to be the whole
material of our knowledge. For instance, in noticing the
constant change, he says, in things around us, we cannot
but observe that new things come into being, and that they
do so as the result of 'the due application and operation of
some other being'.[2] From this observation we get our
ideas of cause and effect; such causation we 'notice' in the
case of creation, generation, and alteration. Clearly Locke
regards the idea of the relation of cause and effect as a
complex idea, and not as a simple idea given in sensation;
he does not maintain that we can actually with our eyes see
a cause causing its effect. But what does he mean by
saying that this relation, like all relations, 'terminates in'
simple ideas? It must be admitted that there is a certain
uncritical vagueness in Locke's treatment of the subject.
In the same way he finds no difficulty in speaking of our
'noticing' persistent identity—'considering anything as
existing at any determined time and place, we compare it
with itself existing at another time, and thereon form the
ideas of *identity* and *diversity*'.[3] But when we turn our
eyes away from an object, how can we tell when we look
again at a later time that it is the same object that we now
see and not a similar one substituted for it? Even if we do
not turn aside our glance, have not skilful substitutions
often deceived the eyes? The truth is that Locke did not
ask himself these questions, and there was much work
left for Berkeley and Hume.

The discussion of the problem of identity does, however,
cause Locke to go farther and deeper into the difficulties
connected with the conception of substance. He now sees
that substance must be thought of not only as the 'some-

[1] *Essay*, II. xxv. 9.   [2] Ibid., xxvi. 1.   [3] Ibid., xxvii. 1.

thing I know not what' in which qualities inhere, but also as the unchangeable permanent which underlies change. It is in this aspect that the problem has been more commonly raised in subsequent philosophy. We have the ideas, says Locke, of three sorts of substances only; of God, of finite intelligences, and of bodies. God is without beginning, eternal, unalterable, and everywhere; and therefore concerning His identity there can be no doubt. With regard to the identity of bodies Locke sees no great difficulty. If two or more atoms be joined together into the same mass, he says, then so long as they exist united together, the mass consisting of the same atoms must be the same mass or the same body, however much the relations between the 'parts' of the body may change; but if one of these atoms be taken away, or one new one added, it is no longer the same mass or the same body. In the case of living creatures identity depends not on a mass of the same particles but on something else. In these the variation of great particles of matter does not alter the identity; an oak growing from a plant to a great tree, and then lopped, is the same oak; and a colt, grown up to a horse, sometimes fat sometimes lean, is all the while the same horse. The reason for this is that in the two cases a mass of matter and a living body identity is 'not applied to the same thing'.[1]

It is to be noticed that Locke does not inquire how it is to be discovered whether what is apparently the same body consists of the same atoms to-day as yesterday, nor does it occur to him to doubt whether this fact is in practice discoverable; nor does he ask how it is to be proved that there is in reality such a thing as an atom—a particle of matter of finite size, which is further indivisible and un-

[1] *Essay*, II. xxvii. 3.

changeable—and that all material inanimate bodies are aggregates of such atoms. All these things Locke takes for granted on the credit of the physical science of his day. Further, if any one wished infallibly to ascertain whether a particular oak grew out of the very acorn which he planted, it is clear that Locke's inquiry into the principles of the 'identity of vegetables' [1] would not practically assist him. However, it is quite true that if I could finally satisfy myself that this pen which I use to-day is an aggregate of the self-same atoms which composed the pen I used yesterday, then I should be finally assured that it is the same pen which I have used on both occasions; moreover it is difficult to see how else I can be assured of this. This, at any rate, is the way in which science attacks the problem, and this fact Locke saw and emphasized. But if this is so, then, even on Locke's showing, more is known about substance than that it is 'something I know not what', since science is continually discovering more about it; scientists are attaining more and more success in explaining change in terms of an unchangeable—and in this part of his argument at least Locke identifies the unchangeable with substance. Unfortunately Locke never expressly states this view; he never tries to put into words the special view of substance implied in his account of the identity of inanimate bodies; probably he did not see that a special view of substance was implied.

In a parallel manner, by psychological inquiry, Locke seeks to discover more about substances of the third kind, namely finite intelligences. It is consciousness, he declares, which makes personal identity.[2] Since consciousness always accompanies thinking, and it is this that constitutes in every one that which he calls 'self', and by this he

[1] See ibid., 4.   [2] Ibid., 9.

distinguishes himself from all other thinking things, in consciousness alone consists personal identity—that is, the sameness of a rational being. As far as this consciousness can be extended backwards to any past action or thought, so far reaches the identity of the person; it is the same self now that it was then. This view seems to imply that if I am conscious of having done a thing then it was I who did it; if I am not conscious of having done it, then, though it was done, it was not I who did it. Locke admits that there are difficulties in this account of personal identity; but these difficulties he says must not unduly worry us, since we may trust that God in His goodness, where the happiness or misery of any of his creatures is concerned, will not 'by a fatal error of theirs transfer from one to another that consciousness which draws reward or punishment with it.' [1] This appeal to the goodness of God at least shows that Locke realized the great difficulties which stand in the way of the apprehension of the personal identity of rational beings; he further hints that the difficulties are insuperable.

Locke now considers that he has given a satisfactory account of the way in which we come by all the knowledge and beliefs which we have; he claims to have shown that there is no need to believe in innate ideas, since all our knowledge has been demonstrated to have been derived from simple sense-perception and reflection on sense-perception; and he has set out in order the way in which these things happen. It now remains for him to carry out the second part of his professed design—to determine the extent and validity of human knowledge. Now that he has discovered the way in which knowledge comes into being, it should be quite a simple matter, he thinks, to estimate its worth when fully developed.

[1] *Essay*, ii. xxvii. 13.

Knowledge is nothing, he says, but 'the perception of the connexion and agreement, or disagreement and repugnancy of any of our ideas'.[1] Where this perception is, there is knowledge; and where it is not, though we may fancy, guess or believe, yet we always come short of knowledge. The differences in clearness in knowledge seem to be due to different ways of perception which the mind has of the agreement or disagreement of any of its ideas. Sometimes the mind perceives the agreement or disagreement of two ideas immediately, without intervention of any other; this we may call *intuitive* knowledge, e.g. that white is not black, that a circle is not a triangle, that three are more than two and equal to one and two. This kind of knowledge is 'the clearest and most certain that human frailty is capable of'; it is irresistible, and 'like bright sunshine forces itself immediately to be perceived as soon as ever the mind turns its view that way'.[2] On this intuition only depends all the certainty that we have in knowledge. If we demand a greater certainty than this, Locke says, we demand we know not what, and show only that we have a mind to be sceptics without being able to be so.

The next degree of knowledge is where the mind proceeds to discover the agreement or disagreement of two ideas by the intervention of other ideas—one or more, as it happens; this kind is called *demonstrative* knowledge. This knowledge, though certain, is not so easily come by; a steady application and pursuit is required for its discovery. Each step in demonstration must have intuitive evidence, since without such perception of agreement there is no new knowledge produced. It has been generally taken for granted, Locke says, that mathematics alone are capable of demonstrative certainty; but this may possibly

[1] *Essay*, IV. i. 2.   [2] Ibid., ii. 1.

be due to the want of method and application in us and not of sufficient evidence in things; demonstrative knowledge has been scarcely so much as aimed at by any but mathematicians, so that we cannot well assert that it is elsewhere impossible. Locke himself thinks that the problems of morality should prove capable of demonstrative treatment.

These two kinds, intuitive and demonstrative, are the only kinds of *knowledge* properly so-called. Sensitive knowledge of particular existences only 'passes under the name of knowledge;'[1] it goes beyond 'bare probability', but does not reach perfectly to the foregoing degree of certainty. Of the existence of particular ideas in the mind we have intuitive knowledge; but whether in any particular case there is outside our minds a real object which the idea resembles is held by some men, says Locke, to be open to doubt, since such an idea may sometimes arise in the mind when no such real object exists. This scepticism with regard to particular perceptions is unavoidable, in view of past deceptions; but with regard to the existence of bodies in general Locke holds such a doubt to be unreasonable, on the ground that there is as clear a difference between an idea of sense and an idea of memory or imagination as there is between two distinct ideas;[2] our certainty of the existence of bodies is in fact 'as great as our happiness or misery, beyond which we have no concernment to know or to be'.[3] Yet the mere appearance of the doubt shows that this is not really knowledge, in the proper sense of the word.

The extent of our knowledge thus falls short, not only

[1] *Essay*, IV. ii. 14.
[2] Hume agrees with Locke that there is a recognizable difference between perception and memory or imagination—they *feel* different; but he sees that this does not prove the independent existence of a physical world. [3] *Essay*, IV. ii. 14.

of the real nature of things, but even of the extent of our own ideas. We have many ideas about which we shall perhaps never have knowledge. The simple ideas, for instance, of which our complex ideas of substances are made up, are for the most part 'such as carry with them, in their own nature, no visible necessary connexion or inconsistency with any other simple ideas.'[1] It is in vain therefore that we endeavour to discover by our ideas (the only true way of certain and universal knowledge) what other ideas are to be found constantly conjoined in our complex ideas of substances, since we neither know the real constitution of the minute parts on which their qualities do depend, nor, did we know them, could we discover any necessary connexion between them and any of the secondary qualities. The conclusion is that however many and various may be the qualities which we apprehend by sense, we can never have knowledge strictly speaking of any real thing, since we can never be assured of any real or necessary connexion between the qualities apprehended. Our knowledge in this sphere 'reaches very little farther than our experience';[2] that is to say, since experience makes us aware of qualities but does not assure us of connexions between qualities, it can give us no knowledge of particular substances at all.

Thus our ignorance is great, greater than our knowledge. Of our own existence it is true we have intuitive knowledge, and of God's demonstrative knowledge; but of the existence of other things, we have only this 'sensitive knowledge', by courtesy so-called. The precise nature and value of this 'sensitive knowledge' on Locke's view is not easy to determine. He sometimes speaks as if we could be quite sure of the independent existence of any given body when we are actually perceiving it. 'No particular

[1] Ibid., iii. 10.   [2] Ibid., 14.

man', he says, 'can know the existence of any other being, but only when by actual operating upon him it makes itself perceived by him'; and again, 'it is therefore the *actual receiving of ideas from without* that gives us notice of the existence of other things'.[1] But this cannot be Locke's real view; he himself insists on the fact that the evidence of particular sense-perception is inadequate evidence for the existence of bodies, and he points out that the having the idea of anything in our minds no more proves the existence of that thing than 'the picture of a man evidences his being in the world, or the visions of a dream make thereby a true history'.[2] In fact, Locke fully admits that the evidence for the existence of external bodies will not survive criticism, if any one is sceptic enough to criticize it. No doubt he regards such criticism as silly, except in the case of secondary qualities; but in truth it is no more silly to doubt the reality of primary than of secondary qualities.

What then are we to say of physics and the other empirical sciences if we admit that they cannot give us certain knowledge? What exactly is this 'sensitive knowledge' of which Locke speaks? It must be admitted that Locke's account of it is not very detailed or careful; perhaps because he thought it to be his business as a philosopher to give his attention primarily to knowledge proper. He tells us that he 'suspects' that natural philosophy can never be made a science. The most that can be expected is that we may have 'experiments and historical observations', from which we may 'draw advantages of ease and health, and thereby increase our stock of conveniences for this life'.[3] This seems to mean that while we cannot delve beneath the

---

[1] *Essay*, IV. xi. 1–2. Italics mine. It will be remembered that Reid revives this doctrine in his argument against Hume.

[2] Ibid.   [3] Ibid., xii. 10.

surface to lay bare the real nature of things, yet we can in a superficial manner gain some acquaintance with the behaviour of things as affecting us, and so learn to accommodate ourselves to their behaviour for our greater comfort. Beyond this our talents reach not; but we may comfort ourselves with the reflection that this is all that our state requires.

The way of true knowledge is of course quite other than the way of 'natural philosophy', which we have just been examining; but here also Locke's account is very short and meagre. The true method of advancing knowledge is by considering our *abstract ideas*. In this way, as we learn from the mathematicians, we may have certain knowledge; in mathematics we proceed to the discovery and demonstration of truths that appear at first sight beyond human capacity. Locke of course repudiates the view that the certainty and accuracy of mathematics are due to the fact that the propositions are arrived at by deduction from *praecognita* [1]—simple foreknown first principles; he attributes their certainty to the clearness, distinctness, and completeness of the ideas with which they are concerned. Our idea of a triangle as a plane figure with three sides, though derived from and essentially dependent upon sense experience, is yet so clear and complete that we can see that it *cannot* have three sides without also having three angles, neither more nor less. Of course Locke, empiricist though he is, does not maintain that we *actually see* with our bodily eyes the necessity of its having three angles; but he thinks the empirical origin of this truth is sufficiently safeguarded by the fact that the idea of a triangle is derived from sense-experience; the 'seeing' of the necessity therefore may safely be attributed to intuition.

[1] Ibid., 1.

Knowledge then, strictly so called, is possible, according to Locke, when sense-perception provides us with ideas such that necessary relations between them can be intuited or demonstrated. In the case of the great majority of our ideas this is not possible; but in some cases, notably mathematics, it is possible and can produce 'wonderful and unexpected discoveries'.[1] Locke always speaks of mathematics as of a great mystery, of which he has but little understanding, and his references to the methods employed are very general and cautious; he tells us that they are 'to be learned in the schools of the mathematicians',[2] and has very little else to say about them. Thus in the case of the only science which on his own showing has produced knowledge in the strict sense his critical inquiry is not profound. He simply asserts that this knowledge does not depend upon deduction from simple general principles, given before birth or by revelation, but upon the examination and comparison of ideas derived from experience. By attending to the ideas which we have of e.g. a straight line, a plane surface, a triangle—ideas which were in the first instance derived from sense-perception—we can pass on to discover by intuition necessary relations between them, and so extend our knowledge. Locke does not inquire in any detail how we do this, nor does he ask himself what reasonable ground we can have for believing in the infallibility of these intuitions. He simply notices that in mathematics we are able to follow this method with satisfying results, whereas in other spheres (excepting perhaps the case of morality) we cannot.[3]

Clearly the essential point here is that Locke thought

---

[1] *Essay*, IV. xii. 7.　　　　　　　　　　　　　　　[2] Ibid.

[3] It remained for Berkeley to get into difficulties by pursuing this inquiry in detail. See pp. 87–96.

that he could work out an account of knowledge, satisfactory on his own empirical principles, without essentially differing from the current theory of thinking—in other words, without turning his back on the current logic. It never seems to have occurred to him to doubt that thinking consists in examining our ideas and bringing out by close analysis what is contained in them. Mathematics is in this respect the crowning instance, he thought, of thinking at its best, and is thus the type of knowledge properly so called. This is to say that thinking is analytical; it analyses ideas, and only finds in them (if it is really thinking, and not a spurious counterfeit) what is there to be found. This being so Locke's only task as an empirical philosopher was, as he conceived, to show that the ideas which thought analyses were not of any mysterious or transcendental origin, but were given in conscious experience—that is, given to sense. Taking it then that mathematical thought consists in analysing certain ideas, e.g. of a triangle, he just thought to show that these ideas arose from sense-perception. Seeing that his position was in general obviously sound, he unfortunately gave very little attention to the detailed consideration of whether the ideas which are given in sense will suffice alone as the datum for thought. It was left to Berkeley to draw attention to the fact that Locke's theory of mathematical knowledge really rests on the assumption that through perception we are given *abstract* ideas, and that this is certainly not the case. This, as both Berkeley and Hume saw, meant that the empirical philosophy must work out a new theory of thinking.

With regard to his theory of such science as is not mathematical, it hardly needs to be said that Locke was clearly a sceptic, wanting only the will to put his conclusions in a sceptical form. He recognized that of the conclusions of such science no man can be rationally convinced; and so he implies that our practical conviction of them, which he recognizes—in other words the fact that we behave as if we were convinced—must be attributed to other causes. In this sphere, Hume with his naturalistic explanation of human belief and behaviour was his inevitable successor. The fact that Locke stopped half-way seems to have been due to his affection for common sense: he stood in the position of the practical man, who, recognizing that for one reason or another a particular problem cannot be argued right out, accepts a particular argument as not final certainly, but 'good enough'. And Locke left it at that; he lacked the remorseless logic to urge that what is just not proved is not known; and that where there is *no* knowledge there can be no probability.

Yet if we consider Locke's most cautious estimate of the results of his inquiry in the *Essay*, his attempt to show that knowledge is derived from experience seems to be sound as far as it goes; though perhaps it may appear that, apart from indeed sweeping away much 'rubbish on the road to knowledge', it does not go very far. His philosophy, rightly regarded, provides not a theory of knowledge, but the beginnings or groundwork of a theory of knowledge. He was right in pointing out that all knowledge and all beliefs take their rise in experience *somewhere*; but in the case of much of our knowledge, subsequent philosophy has shown it to be a far more difficult task than Locke realized to determine just on what experience particular truths are based. Locke shows that the really vital step on the road to knowledge is the discovery of a necessary connexion between our ideas, since it is this step which distinguishes true knowledge from mere belief. He does not notice, however, that this step has not been shown by him to be derivable from experience at all. The ideas themselves are no doubt dependent upon sense-perception, but the discovery of necessary connexions between them is not itself an act of sense-perception, nor has it even been shown by Locke to be necessarily accompanied or conditioned by any such act. Unless it can be shown that this vital operation is itself dependent upon an act of sense-perception, then experience provides the merest *occasion* for the discovery of mathematical truths, and the empiricist has advanced his claims no farther. Thus, as a constructive thinker, Locke leaves his task essentially uncompleted. The philosopher who, like Spinoza or Leibniz, believes primarily in mathematical thinking will still, for all that Locke has said, repudiate sense-perception on the ground that the vital processes in knowledge are non-sensitive; while he who, like Hume, believes primarily in sense-perception will still reject mathematics, and with it all that Locke would call real knowledge, as making assertions which perception through the senses can never justify.

3. *Moral and Political Theory.*

The special views of Locke in moral and political theory may be said to centre in his lifelong enthusiasm for toleration and the freedom of the individual. In the *Essay* Locke was writing for a world which was prepared to have the scope of its inquiring and its questioning limited by authority; and he wrote to protest against this limit to the freedom of thought. Similarly in religious matters Locke found the world ready to consent to persecution as necessary and natural. So far the doctrines of the Reformation asserting the freedom of the Christian man had not meant freedom of the individual from persecution for his religious beliefs. Rather the struggle to maintain new beliefs against hostile authorities and the natural inertia of human nature had promoted and developed strong and varied sectarian consciousness, which chiefly tended to multiply the grounds and occasions for religious persecution. It was recognized that the doctrines of Christianity represented mankind as ideally a close and intimate brotherhood, and every new sect was called into being by the belief that its own founders had at last found the true principles of communion; so there naturally went in company with an earnest faith in the particular new principle a fierce determination at all costs to spread and promote this true brotherhood upon earth.

It is against this attitude of mind, which he found to be permeating Christendom as a whole, that Locke set out to write. Brought up in Puritan surroundings, Locke must at Oxford have come to some extent under the influence of Owen, the Puritan Tolerationist. But Locke's advocacy of toleration was broader and more liberal than Owen's. The latter defended liberty of different religions within the same nation, but as a member of a separatist sect was averse to the attempt to comprehend wide differences of opinion within the same ecclesiastical community. Locke on the other hand wished that men should live in the spirit in which on his death-bed he declared himself to be dying—'in perfect charity with all men, and in sincere communion with the whole church of Christ, by whatever names Christ's followers choose to call themselves'.[1] Locke regards it as the essence of Christianity that Christians should mutually tolerate one another. 'Absolute liberty', he says, 'just and true liberty, equal and impartial liberty, is the thing we stand in need of.'[2]

[1] Quoted by A. C. Fraser, *Locke*, p. 270.
[2] Cf. ibid., p. 94.

In the *Epistola de Tolerantia*, published anonymously in Latin in 1690, a few months before the *Essay*, Locke gives a lengthy vindication of his wide views of religious toleration. These arguments have had so much to do with the formation of the views of the modern world in this connexion that they now appear platitudinous, long-winded, and tedious. No man is hurt, he says, because his neighbour is of a different religion; indeed when we think of the small amount of certainty which we have in matters of religious belief, we should rather think that these differences should be encouraged, since they tend to develop the intellectual resources of mankind in the discovery of the truth, so that men are thereby benefited. In any case, physical punishment is not a possible means of bringing the truth to individuals; even where it secures outward conformity it can but be making men into hypocrites. A man can only believe when provided with sufficient evidence, and where we cannot convince our neighbour by evidence, we should recognize the uncertainty of our own belief and welcome inquiry after truth along a different road. The Christian faith must in the end, Locke urges, be reasonable, and must stand by virtue of reasoned defence, not by force and persecution. He admits that we are as yet far from fully comprehending it. In his work on *The Reasonableness of Christianity* he emphasizes that natural religion is founded on the reason; it is extended by revelation, but reason must constantly control our faith in revelation, and faith cannot convince us of anything contrary to reason. Thus there is little that we know as yet and much which needs to be known, so that mankind cannot but gain by the freedom of the inquiring spirit in religious matters.

Toleration, however, should have its limits. These

limits were set in Locke's mind partly by his practical
common sense in facing the problems of politics, and
partly by his special view of morality. He saw clearly the
practical impossibility of that absolute and universal
toleration which Plato pictures in his caricature of democracy. But apart from its impracticability, Locke thought
such an ideal was excluded on moral grounds. In dealing
with morality he did not stand by his general view of the
relativity and uncertainty of human knowledge. Moral
questions, he thought, admit of being determined with
certainty, and moral philosophy should be capable of
becoming a demonstrative and exact science like mathematics. How Locke would have worked out his moral
system, had he accepted the task urged upon him by his
friend Molyneux, it is impossible to determine with
assurance. Certainly he thought that the primary duty of
man is to seek happiness and avoid misery, and certainly
he thought of happiness in terms of pleasures; and it never
occurred to him to doubt whether happiness is the highest
possible aim of man. Probably therefore his moral theory
when worked out would have been not unlike the utilitarian system developed by Bentham a century later.
Certainly Locke's view is the same as Bentham's in regard
to the bearing of morality on politics. Every man is to
count as one, and no one is to count as more than one;
no man can be allowed to interfere with the freedom of
another, and even theories or religious beliefs which tend
to induce their votaries to attempt to force their views on
their neighbours, or in any way to interfere with the
independence of other people, cannot at any cost be
tolerated in society. Such people fall outside the pale of
toleration. Thus it has been said in regard to Locke that
'not only Catholicism and Protestantism but Rationalism

also has its intolerance'. Whether or not this may fairly be called intolerance, certainly Locke's moral views provided a firm and inviolable dogma upon which his political views were based.

In the *Two Treatises of Government* Locke's declared intention was 'to establish the throne of our great restorer, our present king William; to make good his title in the consent of the people; which, being our only one of all lawful governments, he has more fully and clearly than any prince in Christendom; and to justify to the world the people of England, whose love of their just and natural rights, with their resolution to preserve them, saved the nation when it was on the very brink of slavery and ruin'.[1] Like Hobbes, Locke bases the obligation to obey the State on the supposed fact that the State was in the first place a voluntary institution, formed by a covenant of every man with every man; he too feels that the wide sacrifices of natural rights made by the citizen are only justifiable if they were in the first place voluntary. Unlike Hobbes, he does not think that the State is necessary to make man moral; even in the state of nature, according to Locke, man could recognize duties—for instance the duty not to interfere on insufficient reason with the freedom of his neighbour. Before men could live together in peace and quiet, however, they needed a judge to settle their disputes, and agreed and firmly sanctioned principles according to which they should be settled. To this end they made a covenant and formed a civil society.

According to Hobbes, the only safe way of securing the stability of the State, granted the self-seeking nature of mankind, was that all should agree to transfer supreme power, indivisible and inalienable, to a sovereign, and

[1] *Two Treatises of Government*, Preface.

should renounce once and for all the right to take that power away from him or to interfere in any way with the exercise of it. On this view he who did so interfere would be a rebel against the covenant and thereby outlawed by all who were parties to the covenant. Thus those who caused James II to be deposed in 1688, and set up William and Mary, were according to these principles not defenders of the commonwealth of England against a tyrant, but rebels against the State; moreover on this view the covenant was broken by the Revolution and the civil state of England dissolved. This Locke thought to be nonsense. Clearly the continuity of the existence of the State was not broken by the change of monarch in 1688. According to Locke the true view is that the sovereign willed that the form of government should be changed, and that the legislative, executive, and administrative, instead of residing in the sole person of James II, should reside in William and Mary in Parliament—the sovereign being that on which the credit and stability of governments depend, that is the will of the people.

Thus the fundamental principle of democracy is clearly stated in Locke, though his vindication of it was not so much due to an explicit desire to champion the democratic ideal as to a plain attempt to understand what had happened in 1688. He felt that the change that had then occurred was right and good, and constituted a real political advance; and he wished to demonstrate that this was so and to explain what it was in principle which made it so. This strong practical element in Locke's inquiry, which may be contrasted with the more imaginative and fundamental speculations of Rousseau, explains how it was that his theory exercised so great an influence on the political practice of succeeding generations. Montesquieu was a follower of Locke; and the founders of the North American constitution owed most of their political theory to Montesquieu, and much of their language to Locke himself. A modern writer has said: 'The constitutional life of modern states is essentially based on Locke's principles; the limits of his whole philosophy of the state coincide with the limits of the constitutional question.'

Behind this rises the social question. Here also Locke in his second *Treatise* has made the most pregnant suggestion ever offered by any writer. His theory of the origin of the right of property 'has all but completely established the fundamental principle which lies at the bottom of the science of wealth'.[1] Although three-quarters of a century elapsed before the importance of his doctrine came to be fully recognized, its influence can readily be traced in the classical economists, and since the writings of Karl Marx it has assumed first-rate importance as the main principle lying at the root of Socialistic theory.

In the first place, says Locke, the earth and all inferior creatures were held in common by all men; each man had as 'property' only his own person, the labour of his body, and the work of his hands. But when a man by his own effort has changed a thing from the state in which nature made it, that thing from being common becomes the property of him that mixed his labour with it. 'Thus this law of reason makes the deer that Indian's who hath killed it; it is allowed his goods who hath bestowed his labour upon it, though, before, it was the common right of every one.'[2] This right of property is a right assigned by Nature; it requires no government to establish it, nor can any government take it away. But reason assigns a natural

[1] McCulloch: quoted by A. C. Fraser, *Locke*, p. 102.
[2] *Two Treatises of Government*, ii. 30.

limit to the application of this principle. As much as any one can make use of to advantage of life or comfort before it spoils, so much he may by his labour fix his property in. Beyond this he may not go; nothing was made by God for man to spoil or destroy. Considering the great natural wealth of the world, Locke thinks, and the fewness of the spenders and consumers, there cannot well be ground for quarrel; there must always be raw material somewhere which a man may by his labour make his own.

It is clear that Locke did not consider the possibility of a state of affairs like the present in which there is little or no product of nature which is not, under the sanction of the established order, the property of some one, so that a man may easily die of starvation before he can reach any unappropriated material which he can by labour make his own. While Locke's principle had shown itself to be the fruitful seed from which have grown many different solutions of the problem, none of these solutions can be reasonably attributed to Locke himself. One thing is clear; in this as in other cases Locke was led to oversimplify the problem. He thought that the distribution of property and wealth was easily and perfectly controlled by nature herself, and that in this sphere the exercise of human ingenuity and organization was not required. In this he was the true forerunner of the *laissez-faire* economists and politicians. Indeed, on this as on other points, the main trend of English thought in the first three-quarters of the nineteenth century is towards the making explicit and developing of doctrines which are plainly implicit in the philosophy of Locke.

BERKELEY

1. *Life.*

GEORGE BERKELEY was born at Dysert Castle, county Kilkenny, Ireland, on 12 March 1685. His parents seem to have been in no way remarkable; his family was not wealthy, but was recognized as of gentle blood. He was educated at Kilkenny School, where Congreve and Swift had been twenty years before him; Thomas Prior, his lifelong friend and correspondent, was his schoolfellow. Little is known of his school-days, though tradition not unnaturally says that he was a creature of airy visions and romance. In 1700 he entered Trinity College, Dublin, and he remained there continuously, first as scholar and later as fellow and tutor, for thirteen years. Those years were his most striking period of literary activity. In 1707 he published two mathematical tracts in Latin—*Arithmetica* and *Miscellanea Mathematica*. Two years later appeared his *Essay towards a New Theory of Vision*; while in 1710, when he was twenty-five years of age, there burst upon the world fully fledged his whole philosophy of the universe in Part I of a *Treatise concerning the Principles of Human Knowledge, wherein the chief causes of error and difficulty in the Sciences, with the grounds of Scepticism, Atheism, and Irreligion, are inquired into.* In 1713, when he left Dublin, one of his aims was to attend to the printing in London of his *Three Dialogues between Hylas and Philonous.* At this time, his metaphysical views were received with ridicule, though Lord Pembroke, to whom Locke's *Essay* had been addressed, 'thought the author an ingenious man and to be encouraged'.

The next eight years were spent between London, France, and Italy (where on a second visit he remained four years). In London he at once became friends with Steele, Addison, and Swift, and their circle. He seems to have written little during this period; he probably did some work on the second part of the *Principles*, but later the manuscript was lost and he could not bring himself to write it again. He collected materials for a natural history of Sicily, but this manuscript also was lost. His journal, written in Italy, survives, and shows a continuous and lively interest in natural beauty and in art. In 1720 he wrote in Latin the *De Motu*, and published it a year later.

On his return to England in 1720, Berkeley's interest was at once turned to social questions. The country was disturbed by the misery and social unrest consequent on the failure of the South Sea Company, and Berkeley's imaginative mind saw as underlying this distress a grave decline in public morals. He wrote an *Essay towards preventing the ruin of Great Britain*, which was published anonymously in 1721; and, perhaps because of his dissatisfaction with conditions at home, he became at this time enthusiastically interested in a plan to found a college in the Bermudas. This scheme had as its twofold purpose 'the reformation of manners among the English in our western plantations, and the propagation of the Gospel among the American savages'. When in 1724 he was presented to the rich and influential deanery of Derry, he welcomed the preferment on account of the assistance the position would afford him in promoting this scheme.

Berkeley now spent four years in London in endeavouring to extract a charter and a grant of money for the founding of his college. So persuasive was his charm that Bermuda became the 'fashion' in London; he raised a considerable sum by private subscription, and secured the passing of a vote of £20,000 in the Commons. After waiting for some time for the money to be paid, he set sail privately from Greenwich with his newly married wife in September 1728. He remained for three years at Newport, Rhode Island, and exercised some permanent influence on American philosophy and education through his intercourse with Jonathan Edwards, the Maryland philosopher. At last, he gave up all hope of receiving the grant, and returned to London in 1732, where he remained for two years, publishing *Alciphron* in 1732, the *Theory of Vision or Visual Language vindicated and explained* in 1733, and the *Analyst* in 1734. His defence of religion in *Alciphron* made some stir at the time, but the visual language theory met with little acceptance and much ridicule.

In 1734 Berkeley returned to Ireland as Bishop of Cloyne, where he remained in almost unbroken seclusion for eighteen years. Here he resumed study 'with unabated attention', but his health was indifferent. About this time his metaphysical views began to receive more serious treatment; five years later, with the publishing of the *Treatise of Human Nature*, came Hume's unstinted tribute—'A great philosopher (Dr. Berkeley) has disputed the received opinion in this particular, and has asserted that all general ideas are nothing but particular ones. . . . I look upon this to be one of the greatest and most valuable discoveries that has been made of late years in the republic of letters.'[1] Curiously enough, there is no sign that Berkeley himself ever even heard of Hume.

In the years following his mind was much occupied with the widespread suffering caused by famine and disease in Ireland, and he spent his energy in seeking for remedies. His research led him to attribute great virtue to the use of tar-water as a panacea for all bodily ills. In *Siris*, published

[1] *Treatise of Human Nature*, I. i. 7.

in 1744, he expounds the healing properties of tar, with practical hints as to its use, and uses this as an occasion for a final exposition of his metaphysical and religious views. This book made more noise at the time of its appearance than any of his works; but its philosophical importance was concealed behind its promise to mankind of immunity from disease. It remained nevertheless Berkeley's final attempt to express his whole conception of the universe. In it the bold confidence of the *Principles* has entirely disappeared, and its place is taken by the quiet and recondite reflections of a scholar and a recluse. For all that it represents in a real sense the culmination of Berkeley's thought.

Meanwhile Berkeley was taking a great interest in the social and ecclesiastical affairs of his diocese. On the occasion of the Rising in 1745, he wrote a characteristically humane *Letter to the Roman Catholics of Cloyne*; this was followed in 1749 by an *Exhortation to the Catholic Clergy of Ireland*, in a similarly liberal spirit. The habit of studious retirement grew upon him, and when his friends urged his claims to the Primacy, he was unwilling. 'For my own private satisfaction,' he wrote, 'I had rather be master of my time than wear a diadem'.[1] In 1752 he left Cloyne for Oxford, to which he had for a long time looked as an ideal home for his old age. Here, in a house in Holywell Street, he seems to have recovered his health for a time and to have resumed his studies. But on Sunday, 14 January 1753, 'suddenly, and without the least previous notice or pain',[2] he died. He was buried in the Cathedral of Christ Church in Oxford.

[1] Quoted by A. C. Fraser (Oxford edition of Berkeley's *Works*, i. lxxxiv).

[2] Ibid., i. lxxxvii.

Berkeley's charm and the beauty of his character seem to have secured the affection of almost everybody whom he met. The 'fastidious and turbulent' Atterbury is reported to have said of him—'so much understanding, so much knowledge, so much innocence, and such humility, I did not think had been the portion of any but angels till I saw this gentleman.'[1] A few years later Pope paid him tribute in the lines—

> Even in a bishop I can spy desert;
> Secker is decent; Rundle has a heart:
> Manners with candour are to Benson given,
> To Berkeley—every virtue under heaven.[2]

It has fairly been said of him that he was 'one of the most perfect characters among men of letters'.[3]

2. *Theory of Knowledge*

Of all philosophers Berkeley was perhaps by nature the most confident. He claimed to have discovered a New Principle which would solve all problems and confute all heresy, and he seems rarely to have had serious doubts of its efficacy. He expounded his system boldly and shortly, offering in the first place very few arguments in support of it except that of its obviousness. He was well aware of the difficulties caused in the minds of men by the new discoveries of science; he sympathized with those who felt that it was now impossible to credit the existence of a world such as their fathers had believed in, and who having lost their old faiths found it impossible to preserve themselves from complete scepticism. His aim in writing was to show

---

[1] Quoted by A. C. Fraser (op. cit. i. xxxix).   [2] Ibid. lxxiii.
[3] W. R. Sorley, *A History of English Philosophy*, p. 134. For a rather different view of Berkeley's character see G. A. Johnston, *The Development of Berkeley's Philosophy*, p. 334.

that heretical conclusions were not required by the new discoveries, and that old beliefs could exist side by side with
a knowledge of the physical nature of the universe as now
expounded by science. Since it could be shown that science
overstepped its bounds when it asserted that the world
was capable of explanation in terms of materialism, it was
still open to man to believe in the ultimate control of the
universe by a divine and beneficent Spirit.

Thus Berkeley's philosophic life consisted of a never-
ending war with the rationalistic supporters of materialism,
whom he commonly calls Minute Philosophers. In conducting this attack he showed an unquenchable determination to understand his opponents' point of view, and
to meet and refute them on their own ground, and he was
led in this way to neglect the work of clearing up and
elaborating his own view. The lasting value of his philosophy is dependent upon his lifelong criticism of materialism, rather than upon any critical defence of the spiritualism in which he always believed. It will be well, however,
before we consider his criticism in detail, first to attempt to
give some general account of his philosophy as a whole,
showing how the parts, negative and positive, fit in together
to make a unity, which is at any rate a confession of faith,
if not a philosophical system.

The prevalent heresy and scepticism of the day was due,
Berkeley thought, to the false conclusions which were
being drawn from the new discoveries of physics. Science
teaches us to distinguish, it was thought, between appearance and reality, illusion and knowledge. It teaches us that
in our old beliefs we have been deceived by appearances,
and that the real nature of the universe which underlies
the appearances is only now being discovered by experiment and thinking. This real nature is not apprehensible

by the senses, but can be known only by the reason, whose supreme exercise is found in mathematics. Our senses only deceive us, and if we would avoid error we must believe nothing on their evidence. All we dare believe in is science, and the complicated operations of thought by which science arrives at its conclusions. It is the free-thinking of science alone, unhampered by the prejudices of the past and the inherent deceptiveness of man's sensuous nature, which gives us truth.

Thus science claims to be the high-priest of ultimate truth, and the Minute Philosophy will brook no challenge from the believers in religion. Furthermore, their doctrine itself, a rigid materialism, is intrinsically one which no man of any religious experience or belief can accept. The claim of rationalism must be met and repudiated; and this task Berkeley thinks himself able to accomplish. In order to show that the reality which lies behind the curtain of sense is spirit, the scientist's claim to have discovered an ultimate non-sensible material reality must be shown to be a false one. Only by religious and moral experience can man penetrate the curtain of sense; science, in spite of its claims, never goes behind the veil, but is dealing all the time with the sensible world—that sensible world which conceals and is supported by the activities of spirit, whose operations are apprehended not through science, but by spiritual experience alone. Berkeley spends very little effort, at first at any rate, in attempting to determine why the physicist's account is ultimately unacceptable as truth; he rather takes this for granted, and sets himself at once to expose the fallacy in the method of the Minute Philosophy.

In considering the physicist's account of the world we must remember, Berkeley urges, that, unlikely as it appears on the face of it, this account depends wholly on the evidence of the senses. Like the plain man, the physicist starts by seeing and touching, and his account of reality is an elaborate superstructure built upon evidence of this kind. Starting from his awareness of *visibilia* and *tangibilia*, he proceeds to the discovery of certain alleged *invisibilia* and *intangibilia*, underlying the world of sense. Eventually he takes up the paradoxical position of asserting the real existence of the *invisibilia* and *intangibilia*, and denying reality to the *visibilia* and *tangibilia*, from awareness of which he started. The sensible world is illusion, he says; the intelligible world of science, insensible through and through, is real.

This position, Berkeley maintains, is unsound; and the general line of his criticism is clear enough. Analysis shows, he argues, that all the conclusions of science rest upon the observations of the senses as an indispensable datum; these observations can never be checked or discredited, except in the limited sense that particular observations can be rejected in the light of other particular observations. Observation of the physical world can never be criticized by pure thought, that is, in particular, by pure mathematics. All thinking about the physical world assumes the validity of observation, and if it doubts the original observations it doubts everything. Thought can never transcend the sensible in regard to the physical world; it serves only as the servant of observation, every fresh act of knowledge being the work of perception. This is Berkeley's *New Principle*, to which he adhered in essence through all his writings. By it he seeks to refute, once and for all, the claim of science to discover the truth about the ultimate nature of reality.

It is evident at once that Berkeley's objection to the

rationalist argument is no merely formal one. The difference of view lies deeper than that; a complete theory of the method of science is involved, a fact which Berkeley fully realized. The rationalist puts his point in this way: we find in experience that observation sometimes tells us things of which we know, on the evidence of mathematics, that they cannot be true; in these cases we repudiate the observation as obviously misleading, and trust mathematics —as Descartes put it, we trust our reason and distrust our senses. The rationalist thus deliberately maintains that on the evidence of pure reason we may discredit the evidence of sense, and he further maintains that in physics we actually do this. Berkeley gives this doctrine the lie direct; he first boldly seeks to show on general grounds that the conclusion is illegitimate; and then through the course of many years he devotes himself to a detailed analysis of mathematics and physics and their methods, in the attempt to prove that the rationalist misunderstands and misrepresents them. The scientific view, he maintains, of the nature and structure of any particular physical object, or of the physical world in general, depends essentially on the observation of its sensible qualities; granted these qualities, its structure is such and such; if its qualities are not as perceived, its structure will be other than we think; if we cannot be sure of our observations, we cannot be sure of its structure. Observation and scientific theory stand or fall together; science can never reject or transcend the evidence of the senses, and however elaborate be the calculations and ratiocinations involved, fresh knowledge of the physical world is the work of perception. This is the essence of Berkeley's argument, and he thus stands as the true follower of Locke. But, reasonable as the view seems, the development of Berkeley's philosophy shows that there are great difficulties in the way of maintaining it.

We must not, however, in this general survey of Berkeley's philosophy, lose sight of the positive side of his teaching. Though he gave most of his life and all his best thought to his attack on the rationalistic position, there is no doubt that in his own mind this work of criticism was a means to an end. He sought to maintain that the true nature of the world around us, which science wrongly claims to apprehend, is revealed to us in spiritual experience; and he believes that his own attack on scientific thinking leaves the validity of this spiritual experience unimpaired. He teaches that the world is in every detail always in the hand of God, and that our ultimate understanding of it depends on our knowledge of God. This knowledge depending as it does on our apprehension of spirit is totally different in kind from our understanding of the physical world; it owes nothing to the senses, but is direct and immediate in character. In this way we know that the world is in essentials as the Christian religion represents it; we know that God orders that physical events shall conform, for our convenience and happiness, to certain laws of nature, and that this conformity, though usual and general, is not quite necessary and universal, God's will being ultimately arbitrary; we know too the duties which are incumbent upon us as God's creatures; though in all respects, God being an infinite Spirit, His ways in the end are inscrutable to us, yet in His goodness He has made it possible for us to have such knowledge as is necessary to our state. Of all this we are assured by our knowledge of the activities of spirit, which is in the end, for Berkeley, the only true knowledge.

Thus Berkeley finds himself with two special theories to

maintain; a special theory of the method of physical science, and a special theory of the nature of our apprehension of spirit and the activities of spirit. In actual fact, he became so much preoccupied with the difficulties of the first that he gave but scant attention to the second. Yet it is on the latter that the essential doctrines of the Idealism with which his name is associated really rest. The truth is that it is rather as an empiricist, following in the steps of Locke, than as an idealist that Berkeley is of importance in the history of philosophy.

We may now turn to a more detailed examination of his thought. We shall first consider at some length those parts of his works which are concerned with his analysis of our experience of the physical world and his attack on materialism; and we shall then examine more shortly his teaching with regard to our knowledge of spirits and his positive doctrines about the spiritual nature of the ultimate reality.

In the *Principles of Human Knowledge* Berkeley opens his criticism of materialism with a vigorous attack on the general doctrine of 'abstract ideas'. To this spurious doctrine, which, he says, is peculiar to the philosophers and unknown to the vulgar, are due all difficulties and all heresies; by it philosophers have first raised a dust and then complain that they cannot see.[1] Even Locke had allowed himself to subscribe in essentials to this pernicious view. According to him, mathematics, which he allows to be the most certain kind of knowledge, proceeds by the examination and analysis of certain abstract ideas with which the mind is said to be provided. In proving a particular proposition we are not thinking of a particular equilateral, isosceles, or scalene triangle, but of triangle in

[1] *Principles*, Introduction, § 3.

general, which is neither equilateral, isosceles, nor scalene.
Keeping before our minds this abstract idea and analysing
it, we are able to prove propositions of all triangles whatsoever, and our knowledge has universal certainty. In
those sciences or inquiries where our mind is not provided
with such abstract ideas, our apprehension fails of this
certainty and can only by courtesy be given the name of
knowledge at all. Knowledge proper, on Locke's view,
comes by way of the analysis of abstract general ideas.

This doctrine Berkeley regards as the source of all evil.
Without pausing at the outset to consider the arguments in
favour of it, he seeks to demolish it by the new psychological method. Let any man search in his own mind, he
says, for any such abstract idea; it will be clear to him that
he cannot under any conditions entertain the idea of a
triangle which is neither large nor small, equilateral,
isosceles, nor scalene, nor any similar abstract idea. There
are no such things in any mind as abstract ideas; therefore
philosophers when they speak of them speak of things
which do not exist, and are therefore convicted of giving a
fictitious account of the mental operations involved in
mathematics and in thinking in general.

In fact, however, this doctrine of abstract ideas is in
essentials a firmly established doctrine, well grounded in
a careful analysis of thought, and Berkeley's crude
psychological attack on it can in itself make very little
headway against it. The strength of the doctrine lies, as
Plato always urged, in the fact that without some such
universal ideas thought would not be possible; thought is
concerned essentially with the universal, and cannot deal
directly with anything individual. So long as this logical
doctrine is left intact, the proving that abstract ideas are
psychologically impossible does not prove that thought

deals only with particular ideas, which is Berkeley's thesis. Moreover, it is doubtful whether, considered psychologically, Berkeley's proof does more than demonstrate the impossibility of an abstract mental image; and it is clear on analysis that this is not sufficient for his purpose. Certainly it is unlikely that either Locke or any other reputable thinker ever believed in any such thing.

These difficulties Berkeley recognized, and he spent many years in the attempt to solve the problems connected with universals. Even in the *Principles* he says that he has no quarrel with universals, thereby showing that he is aware of the difficulties. As a matter of fact, his statement is not true, for he has a quarrel with universals, as we shall see later. His view, properly developed, requires a new logic, in which universals, strictly speaking, play no part at all.[1] But fortunately, in the *Principles*, he does not leave the matter here. He recognizes that he must show that our knowledge of an external world is possible without abstract ideas, and that without success in this positive task, his negative attack has brought him but an empty victory. He therefore turns his attention to prove that all our knowledge of a physical world, even that which we owe to modern science, is arrived at without the use of abstract ideas. He seeks to do this by considering in detail the case of one abstract idea, Matter, which is supposed to be fundamental to physics and to our knowledge of a physical world generally; and to show that we have no idea of any such thing and have therefore no reason for believing in the existence of any such thing.

[1] J. S. Mill is quite right in maintaining that he is a Berkeleyan; and in his account of inference as 'from particular to particular' he ably works out the view of his master. See his *System of Logic*, Bk. II, ch. iv.

Berkeley has little difficulty in showing that the conception of material substance was in the philosophy of Locke no more than an uncriticized survival. Philosophers had always taken it for granted, largely on the credit of Aristotle's logic, that qualities must be supported by some underlying permanent self-subsistent substance, and Locke had concurred in this; but he had agreed that nothing was known of its nature: all he could say of it was that it was 'something I know not what'. Berkeley now goes farther and argues that since we know and can know nothing of its existence, in that there can be no idea of it, we must conclude that it does not exist. At times he urges in addition that the conception of it is self-contradictory; [1] but his chief effort is directed to showing that there is in fact nothing in experience to justify belief in its existence. This he does by arguing that throughout our whole experience of the physical world, we never apprehend anything but sensible qualities and collections of sensible qualities. All we know of things or can know of them is what we perceive by sense; if there were more in things than this, we could not know it. This at once becomes clear, he says, if we consider what is meant by the term 'exists'. When I say that the table I write on exists, I simply mean that I see and feel it; and if I were out of my study I should say it existed—meaning thereby that if I were in my study I might perceive it or that some other person actually does perceive it. 'There was an odour, that is, it was smelled; there was a sound, that is to say, it was heard; a colour or figure, and it was perceived by sight or

[1] He does this when differentiating between material and spiritual substance, rejecting the former conception and defending the latter. See *Third Dialogue between Hylas and Philonous* (Oxford Edition of Berkeley's *Works*, i. 449 seq.)

touch. This is all that I can understand by these and the like expressions.'[1] This doctrine is evidently based on the argument that whenever we are aware of a physical object, introspective analysis shows that there is nothing present in our mind but a number or collection of simple ideas of qualities; and it is taken by Berkeley to prove that knowledge simply consists in the awareness of sensible qualities.

Here Berkeley is brought into conflict with the current view, also supported by Locke, which distinguished between primary and secondary qualities. This view held that some of the qualities of things, such as colour, heat, taste, and smell, have no existence except in being perceived, while other qualities, such as figure and motion, exist in the bodies themselves independently of being perceived. For Berkeley all sensible qualities are equally real or equally ideal. He argues his point quite simply and, from his own point of view, convincingly; that is, he easily shows that the perceived shape of a thing is in the same case with its perceived colour, whether real or unreal. Figure, he urges, cannot be apprehended except as the figure of some body; and a figured body cannot be apprehended except as having some colour; where the figure is, there the colour is also. Is it possible by any abstraction of thought to conceive the extension and motion of a body without its other sensible qualities, to think of a body as of irregular shape and moving at twenty miles an hour, and yet as being neither red, green, blue, nor any colour whatsoever? The whole notion of an *idea* of something which is invisible and intangible is repugnant to good sense. There are no such ideas. Therefore the world as we know it must be visible and tangible, and have the qualities, primary and secondary alike, which sensible objects have: it must

[1] *Principles*, § 3.

be such as to reveal its whole nature, and its true nature, only to the senses.

From this Berkeley draws the striking conclusion that *esse* is *percipere* and *percipi*. The essence of the mind is to perceive, and the essence of the sensible world, which he identifies with the physical or material world, is to be perceived. Having shown, as he thinks, that we never apprehend more in the physical world than we can perceive, he takes this to mean, not merely that there *is* nothing in the physical world except what can be perceived, but that its essence is to be perceived—that it is fully mind-dependent in the sense that it only exists in and by being perceived. 'Some truths there are', he says, 'so near and obvious to the mind that a man need only open his eyes to see them. Such I take this important one to be, viz. that all the choir of heaven and furniture of the earth, in a word all those bodies which compose the mighty frame of the world, have not any subsistence without a mind; that their *being* is to be perceived or known.' [1] He recognizes, indeed, that physical objects have a greater permanence than they could have if they depended for their existence on being perceived by me or by any particular finite mind; and he therefore says that they exist as ideas in the mind of God, the Infinite Spirit. But it is not difficult to see that this view immediately involves great difficulties. If *esse* is *percipi*, then God must be keeping physical objects in existence by constantly *perceiving* them; and it is difficult to see how this view makes *my* perceptual experience any more intelligible. In any case Berkeley is in effect admitting that the physical world exists independently of my mind which is perceiving it here and now.

As a matter of fact Berkeley never works out in any

[1] *Principles*, § 6.

detail the conclusions of the view that *esse* is *percipi*, and it is very difficult to see why he ever held it.[1] Of course he always believed that matter is mind-dependent, in the sense that everything which is not spirit depends wholly for its existence on the activity of spirit, that is, in the end, on the activity of the Infinite Spirit; and he sought to work out a whole philosophy of spirit in support of this belief. But it is obvious in the later works, and only thinly concealed in the *Principles*, that the doctrine that *esse* is *percipi* is a serious hindrance to the development of this view. The true essence of the physical world is on Berkeley's view to manifest the activity of spirit and the goodness of God's will; perception, being strictly not an activity of spirit at all, but a passivity, has really little importance in this connexion. No doubt God was held to arrange our perceptions with an eye to the convenience of our state, and in this sense the nature of the object perceived is dependent on our nature; but for all that ideas depend for their existence, even in the *Principles*, not on the perceiving mind but on the good pleasure of God.

These doctrines, however, and the arguments in favour of them, rather concern Berkeley's own positive view of the nature of the universe, and will be considered later. What concerns us here is not the metaphysical aspects of the view, but the empiricist doctrine that knowledge of the physical world depends ultimately on the senses alone; that is, that as far as the physical world is concerned knowing is

[1] It is clear that Berkeley, while he wishes to distinguish strictly between *percipere* and *intelligere*, has only very general and vague views as to what is meant by *percipere*, except that the act of perception is certainly dependent in some way upon the senses. He also writes as if the contents of the mind of God were fully and immediately known to us, though this is nowhere his explicit view.

perceiving. If we consider the whole continuity of his thought, this is clearly seen to be the keystone of his teaching, as is shown by his never-varying attitude to abstract ideas. In some form or other he always sought to maintain that thought about the sensible world is wholly confined within the limits of sense-perception; though the details of his view change as he seeks to do more justice to the importance of thinking, the essential teaching remains the same.

It is clear, then, that Berkeley's general view involves special theories both about perception and about thought; the assertion that knowing is perceiving needs to be supported by careful analysis both of sense-perception and of thinking. In the *Principles* Berkeley's formulation of his view is mainly determined by his examination, such as it was, of perception; and it was not until after the publication of this, his best-known work, that he really turned his full attention to an examination of the nature of thinking. We must therefore first give some account of his theory of perception.

It is in the *New Theory of Vision*, which is primarily a psychological work, that we find the most detailed account of Berkeley's views concerning perception; and here he is chiefly concerned with an analysis of the way in which we come by our knowledge of space and spatial relations. The method of the work is strictly empirical; the whole argument requires the reader at every point to look into his own mind and examine his own experience. Physiological considerations have no bearing on the inquiry, and for this reason Berkeley rules out the scholastic treatment of the problem as irrelevant. He also repudiates the geometrical optics which had been developed by the Cartesians. This theory maintained that distance is perceived by means of the angle subtended at the eye by the object. Berkeley objects to this theory that it is a mathematical theory and could be fully understood by a person born blind, who had had no experience of seeing; it is therefore abstract and hypothetical, and is not really the theory of vision. The true theory of vision should assume that when we form conclusions as to the size and distance of objects we are concluding from data of which we are immediately aware by sense, and should examine our experience in order to explain our knowledge in terms of conscious perceptions; it should not assume, for any abstract mathematical reason, the existence of experiences of which we are not aware. Its method must therefore be empirical, and cannot be abstract and mathematical. Berkeley therefore attempts himself to form a theory of the perception of distance and magnitude, based solely on the data of actual vision; he simply examines his own visual experience, and appeals to his reader to do the same. This insistence that inquiry into the working of the mind must proceed by the analysis of individual conscious experience marks an epoch in the development of modern psychology.

Two facts, says Berkeley, are agreed upon by all; first that distance itself is invisible, and secondly that the distance of remote objects is not immediately perceived, but is judged on the basis of past experience. As regards the first point, Berkeley does not attempt to prove that distance is not immediately perceived; he takes it for granted as obvious and common to all contemporary speculation on the subject. As regards the second, his own contribution consists in applying this current theory concerning remote objects to all objects, whether near at hand or far away, as against the common view that the magnitude and distance of near objects was perceived by means of the angle subtended. All perception of distance, he maintains, depends upon experience—we recognize by experience a certain correlation between the senses of sight and touch. 'I believe whoever will look narrowly into his own thoughts . . . will agree with me', he says, 'that what he sees only suggests to his understanding that, after having passed a certain distance, to be measured by the motion of his body, which is perceivable by touch, he shall come to perceive such and such tangible ideas, which have been usually connected with such and such visible ideas.' [1] All that we actually *see* with our eyes are the 'primary' [2] or immediate objects of sight, e.g. colour. The other qualities which we apprehend are tangible qualities 'secondarily suggested' by the colour which we see; thus shape, magnitude, position, for instance, are qualities which we conclude from the visible qualities. They are perceived in the same way as shame or anger is seen in the looks of a man. These passions are themselves invisible; they are nevertheless 'let in by the eye along with colours and alterations of countenance which are the immediate object of vision, and which signify them for no other reason than barely because they have been observed to accompany them'. [3] It is curious, Berkeley admits, that all the qualities to which we give the greatest attention in things are not directly seen, but secondarily suggested; but if we examine the facts, we cannot, he maintains, come to any other conclusion.

Berkeley gets into some difficulty, however, when he turns to consider our apprehension of magnitude, and his

[1] *New Theory of Vision*, § 45.

[2] Berkeley's use of the terms 'primary' and 'secondary' in this connexion must not be confused with their use in Locke's distinction between primary and secondary qualities.

[3] *New Theory of Vision*, § 65.

statements are not altogether consistent with what has gone before. Magnitude, he maintains, is *suggested* by what we see, in the same way as distance. It is true that distance may be inferred from magnitude, or magnitude from distance; but, according to Berkeley, either of them can be arrived at independently, suggested by our visual ideas. In the case of magnitude, however, we distinguish between the visible or apparent magnitude, which decreases as the object recedes from us, and the real magnitude, which remains constant. This distinction, which of course Berkeley recognizes, is inconsistent with the view referred to above that distance and magnitude are not visible, but suggested by the visible qualities. In this case what suggests the real magnitude is not some quite different visible quality, as for instance colour in the case of distance, but the visible magnitude. Being unable to deny that magnitude is visible in view of the obvious distinction between visible or apparent and real magnitude, Berkeley tries to maintain the essentials of his view by asserting that visible magnitude is unreal, the tangible magnitude being the real magnitude. He resists the temptation to say that the real magnitude is inferred from a comparison of the data of sight and touch. His view is not that by a correlation of the evidence of the two senses we arrive at the apprehension of magnitude; any such theory, which lays stress on reflection and inference, he distinctly repudiates. His view is the more difficult one that magnitude is directly apprehended by touch—that tangible magnitude is real magnitude—though visual experience can suggest to us what the magnitude would be found to be if we touched the object. He thus speaks in the last resort as if neither distance nor magnitude were themselves visible.

If Berkeley were right in his account of the apprehension

of spatial relations, there could be no good ground for saying that the senses can deceive us about these relations, or
for maintaining that the real distance, magnitude, position,
&c., of objects must be calculated by mathematics. There
would certainly be no need to use our reason to deliver us
from the deceptions of the senses in these matters; for, if
he is right, all these qualities are directly apprehensible by
sense. This is the conclusion which Berkeley himself
appears to have drawn from his analysis. The distinction between apparent and real magnitude is not a
distinction between sensible and intelligible magnitude, but
only between visible and tangible. Here there is no appeal
from the senses to the reason, but a natural inevitable
appeal from one sense to another, with sometimes in addition
a suggestion by that which we have experienced by sense
of something else which we might experience by sense. It
is the same with other qualities—distance, position, &c.
In general, Berkeley seems to have concluded that all
appeals to reason or to mathematical calculation are in like
case; they are seen on analysis to be really appeals to other
sensuous experiences. Some knowledge, it is true, is in
point of fact arrived at by inference, but it could under
other circumstances have been directly given to sense.
The movement of the earth round the sun is in fact inferred; but we might, could we stand on the sun, see it so
moving—this, which we might see, is suggested to us by
what we do see. With other discoveries of science the case
is the same; we can never get away from and beyond the
sensible. All that we do is to infer future or possible sense-
experience from actual sense-experience, and there is no
ground for believing in the existence of anything non-
sensible.

This is the position to which Berkeley seems to have

been led by his inquiry in the *New Theory of Vision*. It is not surprising that when he came to build a theory of knowledge and a system of metaphysic he should maintain that thought in the scientific disciplines merely served the purpose of putting us in the way of new perceptions, and that the whole guarantee of knowledge and the work of adding fresh knowledge was dependent upon acts of sense-perception. This view he does in fact maintain, somewhat crudely and aggressively, in the *Principles of Human Knowledge*. Stated in simple form, it is indeed an attractive view, and on the whole it would seem to justify Berkeley in his claim that common opinion is on his side. No doubt the plain man does think that the main achievement of science is anticipation of perception, and that verification by experience provides the whole guarantee of the truth of scientific theory; that a true theory, when once it is understood, is 'obvious on the face of it', and that it is difficult to understand how men did not see it before, without the help of so much mathematics. But when Berkeley came to analyse more closely the part played in science by thought as distinct from perception, he was forced to admit that thinking would not fit into the place that he here assigns to it. The more he considers the work of the exact sciences, the more importance he attaches to thought and the less weight he gives to crude sense-perception, until in the end he becomes a thorough-going conceptualist.

The truth is that Berkeley's analysis of perception, careful and detailed as it appears, is really a highly specialized and narrow one, and is wholly inadequate to support a general theory of knowledge. In many important and fundamental respects Berkeley has no considered view of perception at all. This becomes abundantly clear if we examine his defence of the principle that *esse* is *percipi* in the *Principles* and the *Dialogues*. In defending his view Berkeley insists that he believes in 'things' as much as any man; he merely asserts that their existence is dependent on their being perceived. This assertion is meaningless unless he maintains that we perceive *things*. Locke's view of course is that we perceive simple qualities and then in some way group these simples together into complex ideas of things. These complex ideas would have no existence without some activity on the part of the individual mind which groups the qualities; their existence is essentially dependent on our reflecting or thinking. Yet Berkeley speaks as if the *esse* of complex ideas of things was to be perceived, that is received by a passive mind. Worse still, even in the case of simple qualities Berkeley's view is by no means clear; to make his view plausible he has to speak as if by touch we *perceived* magnitude directly, the process being a passive one; whereas, when pressed, his view as a psychologist is that we see colour, feel hardness, &c., the primary [1] objects of sense, while the secondary objects are suggested. Strictly speaking Berkeley would be required, if he attended closely to his psychological analysis, to say that spatial relations are apprehended by inference, that is, their *esse* is *intelligi*. What he actually does is to insist that ideas or things are apprehended immediately, no inferential process being involved; that is, he really means what he says when he asserts that *esse* is *percipi*. But it is idle to suppose that this view is supported by Berkeley's admittedly valuable psychological investigations; it is entirely at variance with them. Yet the fact that he had apparently conducted an analysis of perception explains the paradox, that his followers, while claiming to be

[1] Cf. *supra*, p. 80, note 2.

a psychological school and insisting on the importance of perception, grounded their theory of knowledge on a theory of perception which proves unable to stand up to the most elementary psychological analysis.

But Berkeley had too active and honest a mind to rest wholly contented with so crude and confused a view. He soon saw that activity on the part of the mind, and even real constructive operations, are involved in our apprehension of the physical world. His increasing interest in the methods of science showed him that this element of activity was of fundamental importance in knowledge; and all the time the constant need to defend his own spiritualistic view of the universe caused him again and again to make disparaging and impatient remarks about the senses and about those who would believe nothing which they could not verify by sight or touch. It was inevitable that he should modify the view of the *Principles*, even while attempting to remain true to his fundamental empiricism. His first attempt to prove that knowledge is essentially grounded, not in the abstract, but in our sensuous experience of a sensible world, by the crude doctrine that knowing *is* perceiving, soon failed him; and he had to attempt the difficult task of working out a more complicated system, which should do justice to the importance in experience of the active operations of disciplined thinking, without being fundamentally disloyal to Locke and to the New Principle. While this attempt, if compared with that of Kant, may fairly be judged a relative failure, it is well worth consideration, in that certain essential points emerge much more clearly and definitively in Berkeley's treatment than in that of Kant.

To understand Berkeley's account of thinking, we must first go back to his attack on the doctrine of abstract ideas in the Introduction to the *Principles*, where he seems almost to be denying the existence of thought altogether. The common view was that knowledge was dependent upon thinking, and that thinking had as its object abstract or general notions. Even Locke had in the end so far forgotten his empiricism as to maintain that true knowledge consisted in the perception of the agreement and disagreement of our abstract general ideas. As we have seen, Berkeley denies the existence of such abstract ideas; he maintains that the only idea which can be present to the mind is the simple idea of something sensible. He asserts, as Hume has clearly explained, 'that all general ideas are nothing but particular ones, annexed to a certain term, which gives them a more extensive signification, and makes them recall upon occasion other individuals, which are similar to them'.[1] In other words, Berkeley is arguing that there are no proper objects of thinking, as separate and distinct from the objects of perception; that is to say, whether we are thinking or perceiving, the ideas which are present to the mind are, on his view, the same. Since, then, Berkeley clearly thinks of both thinking and perceiving as being the awareness of the succession of ideas in the mind, and since the ideas in both cases are the same, viz. ideas of sensible qualities or things, his view seems really to be that thinking is a form of perceiving. Thus in the *Principles* Berkeley is trying to develop a theory of knowledge which makes knowledge dependent upon perceiving alone; and when he is forced to consider those operations of the mind which are commonly called thinking, and as such distinguished from perceiving, he tries to show that they are wrongly so distinguished, and that while they appear to involve operations different in kind they are really only perceptions thinly disguised.

[1] *Treatise of Human Nature*, I. i. § 7.

It must not be supposed that Berkeley expressly states in the *Principles* that in successfully attacking the doctrine of abstract ideas he is repudiating the existence of all general notions; and therefore the existence of the distinctive activity which we call thinking. Indeed, he asserts the opposite: 'It is, I know,' he says, 'a point much insisted on, that all knowledge and demonstration are about universal notions, to which I fully agree.'[1] But it is clear that this is only lip-service; for Berkeley is committed by his New Principle to deny the existence in the mind of any operation other than perceiving, and therefore to deny that any idea can be present to the mind other than ideas perceived. Not even Berkeley would roundly assert that universal notions can be perceived by sense. The truth is that, as has been well pointed out, it is one thing to admit universals, but quite another to say what they are;[2] and if on his own principles Berkeley set out to explain them, he would be bound to explain them away. When he does come closely to consider what he means by universals, he is led to a position far different from that taken up in the *Principles*.

But before condemning him, let us consider Berkeley's own words more closely, and attempt to determine just what he does here mean by universal. 'An idea,' he says, 'which considered in itself is particular, becomes general, by being made to represent or stand for all other particular ideas of the same sort.'[3] What we have present to our minds, for instance, in proving a particular property of a triangle is not an abstract idea of a triangle which is neither isosceles, equilateral, nor scalene, but rather the idea of a particular triangle, which as a matter of fact has one or

[1] *Principles*, Introduction, § 15.
[2] G. A. Johnston, *The Development of Berkeley's Philosophy*, p. 124.   [3] *Principles*, Introduction, § 12.

other of these three characters. We do not, however, in this operation consider those particular qualities which distinguish this from other triangles (though of course the particular triangle present to our minds has such particular qualities), but rather those general qualities which it has in common with other triangles. Thus the idea of this particular triangle acts as a *sign* which *suggests* to us all other triangles of the same kind. A universal notion is really a particular idea acting as a sign, *representing* to us all other things of the same kind.

Here Berkeley is considering primarily his psychological investigation; noticing first that introspection fails to reveal any abstract idea as present to the mind, he then seeks by the same means to discover exactly what does go on in the mind when we make a geometrical proof. He insists that we are, perceptually or imaginatively, examining a particular sensible figure, and that this experience in some way excites in us an awareness of other figures which are of the same kind. This seems to be all that his psychological investigation reveals to him.

At other times he tries to express his view in terms of logic, but his account is extremely obscure. We may be said to be reasoning on the *name* triangle (as he says in the *Commonplace Book*) or (as he says in the *Principles*) on the *meaning* of triangle. The particular may stand for or represent other particulars, because all have the same meaning; and it is about things which, while particular and different, all have the same meaning that we think. It is this meaning that supplies the element of universality.

These words are not at all clear, and in general it is almost impossible to disentangle the various strands in the beginnings of Berkeley's thought about universals. But two things are clear. He lays great stress on the part played in proof by the examination of the particular sensible figure; and he insists that the thinking involved consists of an awareness of a succession of particular sensible ideas suggested by the observation of the figure. In thinking the mind passes from idea to idea, and each one is revealed by introspection as particular and sensible in character. At no stage does a search of the mind reveal an idea which is not sensible.

Any attempt to explain geometrical proof on these principles was bound to lead Berkeley into difficulties. While laying stress on the importance of the observation of the figure, he had to admit, as we have seen, that the imposition on the mind of a certain discipline was essential to the achievement of the proof. He could not maintain that the proved characteristics of the triangle are *perceived* in the triangle in the sense in which colour is perceived. He recognized that the possibility of proof depended upon our disciplining our minds to treat the figure in a certain way; not merely to gaze at it, but to look for something. I must 'consider the figure merely as triangular';[1] I must constrain myself not to attend to all the particular qualities; and I must notice closely to which qualities I have attended, and to which I have not, that I may know of what kind of triangles my conclusion is true. Unless I can impose this discipline upon myself, then, on Berkeley's own showing, I am incapable of geometrical proof.

It was inevitable that this recognition should profoundly modify Berkeley's attitude to perception. He now saw that apprehension was not a matter of the eye and the sense of touch, but of the mind—and that significant perception was conditioned by certain mental activities. This is quite

[1] *Principles*, Introduction, § 16. This passage was added in the 2nd edition of 1734.

clearly stated in *Alciphron*. Here, treating of the nature of beauty, he canvasses the view that it consists in a symmetry and proportion pleasing to the eye; but he rejects it on the ground that the eye cannot see that a chair is handsome or a door well proportioned. 'The beauty, therefore, or symmetry of a chair', he says, 'cannot be apprehended but by knowing its use, and comparing its figure with that use; which cannot be done by the eye alone, but is the effect of judgment. It is, therefore, one thing to *see* an object, and another to *discern its beauty*.' [1] Similarly with many other characteristics of the physical world, it is one thing to see the object and quite another to discern these qualities.

In the Seventh Dialogue of *Alciphron*, Berkeley returns, with these considerations in mind, to a lengthy discussion of the nature of scientific thinking. While remaining consistent in essentials with his attack on Abstract Ideas in the *Principles*, he shows clearly, especially in view of the alterations in the 3rd edition of 1752,[2] that he is travelling further and further from his earlier crude sensationalism. In meeting the attack of the Minute Philosopher on the absurdity of religious faith, Berkeley seeks to show that there is really much faith not essentially different in kind behind the apparently rigid reasoning of the man of science. To maintain this, he is forced to explain with care and in detail his view of the nature of scientific proof, and he therefore here sets out the general results of his long and diligent investigations into the problems of mathematics and physics, expanding and substantiating them in some detail two years later in the *Analyst* and the *Defence of Free-thinking in Mathematics*. It will readily be seen that, while

---

[1] *Alciphron*, Third Dialogue, § 8.

[2] See especially Oxford Edition of Berkeley's *Works*, ii. 341 and 344.

Berkeley was inspired primarily by a desire to vindicate faith in the Christian religion, his investigation of this problem is of great value in itself as a fair examination of the method of science; and it propounds conclusions which are very much in the spirit of well-known modern theories of science.

It will be well first to summarize briefly Berkeley's main argument in this passage, and then to consider its significance. Alciphron, the Minute Philosopher, has maintained that the supporters of religious faith simply exploit the vulgar tendency to use and be affected by words to which no precise meaning can be attached. This tendency, he urges, is responsible for all mental confusion and superstition. Words, if they are not to deceive us, must stand for clear-cut and definable ideas, as do the fundamental abstract terms of science; it is this clarity and definition which enables science to be the source of truth. It is only necessary, in order to discredit religious faith, to point out that its terms, e.g. 'grace', stand for no such clear-cut ideas, and that therefore their use can only lead to confusion of mind. In maintaining this view, Alciphron is standing upon Aristotle's logic; the first principles in knowledge must be completely known, and definable. Where the fundamental terms are not defined no knowledge can be gained. In answer to this Berkeley maintains, and brilliantly defends, the view that the fundamental terms of science are not different in this respect from those of religion. 'Force', for instance, is in no better case than 'grace', seeing that no clear idea of it can be entertained by the mind. Yet in spite of this, there are many significant and valuable propositions made about 'force', and it cannot be denied that physical science contributes to the sum of human knowledge. We may therefore conclude that it is not essential to significant language or to the discipline pursuit of knowledge that there should be clear-cut and distinct ideas to correspond to all the words used: evidently words must have other uses than to suggest definable ideas. So far Berkeley deliberately takes the line as against science which is more commonly associated with Kant and his followers, and so far he argues his point with more learning and with greater examination of detail. But Berkeley stops here where Kant's constructive work begins; he gives very little attention to determining what is the importance and influence of these terms to which ultimately clear-cut, definable ideas are not attached. Having shown that the concept of force is not definable, he does not explain in detail how such a concept can play a part in disciplined thinking: he is only concerned to argue that the votaries of science have no quarrel with religion on this score, being in the same case themselves.

Now though this point of view at first sight appears strange in Berkeley, it is not difficult to see that there is no lack of continuity in the development of his thought. He maintains his early hostility to the 'abstract ideas' of the rationalists or Minute Philosophers, but he is no longer satisfied with the crude doctrine that knowing is perceiving with which he coquetted in the *Principles*. He is clearly seeking a road half-way between the two extremes. 'It is not', he says, 'by mere contemplation of *particular things*, and much less of their *abstract* general ideas, that the mind makes her progress';[1] and though he comes to no satisfactory positive theory in regard to the exact manner in which the mind does make progress, his careful and detailed investigation, pointed as it is by his clear recogni-

---

[1] *Alciphron*, Seventh Dialogue, § 11.

tion of the difficulty, is perhaps more valuable than if he had. But in order to understand his position as a whole, his theory must be considered.

On Berkeley's view, the general terms in language do not stand for clear-cut ideas of any kind, abstract or otherwise: they represent the use of *signs* by the mind, which used as signs have a very obvious value. As soon as we turn aside from their use as signs in practical and useful activities, and consider academic questions about their intrinsic nature and signification—in other words, as soon as we seek for definitions of fundamental terms—we get at once into difficulties. But this applies to all inquiries. In mathematics the symbols play their part without there being any possibility of offering or exhibiting any such ideas to the mind; for instance, 'the algebraic mark, which denotes the root of a negative square, hath its use in logistic operations, although it be impossible to form an idea of any such quantity'.[1] This applies also in geometry to the difficulties about 'the nature of the angle of contact, the doctrine of proportions, of indivisibles, infinitesimals, and divers other points';[2] and, he has already told us, it applies in mechanics and physics to the notions of force, gravity, reaction, impetus, momentum, conatus, &c. In general, it must be confessed that 'even the mathematical sciences themselves, which above all others are reckoned the most clear and certain, if they are considered, not as instruments to direct our practice, but as speculations to employ our curiosity, will be found to fall short in many instances of those clear and distinct ideas, which, it seems, the minute

[1] Ibid., § 14.
[2] Ibid., § 15. Berkeley shows much industry and ingenuity in working out his view in detail in his mathematical writings. Cf. Johnston, *The Development of Berkeley's Philosophy*, ch. v.

philosophers of this age, whether knowingly or ignorantly, expect and insist upon in the mysteries of religion'.[1]

It is to be noticed that Berkeley turns to account in this connexion his theory of perception, and he still maintains his attack on abstract ideas. The keynote of his criticism of science is still his insistence on the part played in it by sense-perception—theology being, of course, freed from this disability by being ultimately dependent on our know-ledge of spirits. While admitting the importance of signs with their universal character, he insists that these signs have their origin in the senses, thus implying that our knowledge is still limited by our acquaintance with 'apt' signs, i.e. by the senses. 'Nothing', he says, 'is more natural, than to make the things we know a step towards those we do not know.'[2] It is natural to substitute objects which are easily comprehended in place of such as are more subtle, fleeting or difficult to conceive. It is natural to assist the intellect by the imagination, the imagination by sense, and the other senses by sight. Hence figures, metaphors, and types; hence also the use of models and diagrams—'right lines are substituted for time, velocity, and other things of very different natures'.[3] Berkeley notices that the signs must be 'apt' to signify that which they represent; but he does not elaborate the point, or propound any theory about the nature of this aptitude. Indeed, he never works out his doctrine of signs in any detail, though he thinks it to be a point of great importance. What he does seek to prove in detail is that science, in its most significant propositions, uses terms to which there are no clear-cut, definable ideas attached. His own view that these notions, themselves indefinable, are used as signs or symbols, he leaves as hardly more than a tentative sug-

[1] *Alciphron*, Seventh Dialogue, § 14.   [2] Ibid, § 13.   [3] Ibid.

gestion. His immediate point is this: since even in science we believe where we do not understand, using notions of which we have no full comprehension, why cavil at an element of mystery in religion?

This general attitude is maintained in the *Siris*, the last of Berkeley's philosophical writings. No doubt this work is not to be regarded as of first-class philosophical importance. It is rather of the nature of a scrap-book, in which reflections on the most diverse subjects are strung together with very little plan or system. Two-thirds of the work consist of rather disorderly disquisitions on various physical, chemical, and biological problems. Even in the philosophical parts Berkeley is rather occupied in drawing attention in great detail to those doctrines in the works of the ancients of which he approves, than in working out his own constructive views. He shows a wide reading of Plato, and in particular seems to have been much influenced by the examination of perception, and the refutation of the view that knowing is perceiving, in the *Theaetetus*. But for all its incoherence and lack of system, the *Siris* throws an interesting light on the direction in which Berkeley's thought was tending, and shows how very far he had moved from the crude theory of knowledge expounded in the *Principles*.

In the *Siris* he affirms without hesitation, and almost without qualification, that apprehension is the work of the understanding, not of the senses. We know a thing when we understand it, he says; and we understand it when we can interpret or tell what it signifies. Strictly, the sense knows nothing.[1] Indeed, sensible appearances often 'render the aftertask of thought more difficult'.[2] So far does he go that he even seems willing to admit the necessity

[1] *Siris*, § 253.   [2] Ibid., § 264

of abstract ideas. 'The mind, her acts and faculties,' he says, 'furnish a new and distinct class of objects from the contemplation whereof arise certain other notions, principles and verities, so remote from, and even so repugnant to, the first prejudices which surprise the sense of mankind that they may well be excluded from vulgar speech and books, as *abstract* from sensible matters, and more fit for the speculation of truth, the labour and aim of a few, than for the practice of the world, or the subjects of experimental or mechanical enquiry.'[1] In this passage Berkeley seems to admit that the fundamental conceptions with which science deals are not of sensible origin; he appears to be tempted to develop the view, of which there are some indications in the *Principles*, that they are dependent upon our awareness of our own mental activities; that is to say, they take their rise, not in ideas at all, but in our notions of spirit. On this view, thinking depends on our apprehension of spirit— the knower, not the known. This is really to abandon empiricism altogether, and would lead directly to the inquiry undertaken by Kant in his *Critique of Pure Reason*.

It is doubtful, however, whether this ever became in any sense Berkeley's official doctrine, or whether he realized in any degree the consequences of it. At any rate it never led him to change his attitude to science. While he admits that science apprehends what it apprehends rather by intellect than by sense, he still will not allow that it apprehends the true nature of reality. This is reserved for philosophy, which he seems not to distinguish from theology. Science proceeds by a kind of 'natural vaticination',[2] without any understanding of causes. It is only in the light of spiritual experience—that is, in the end, religious experience—that the true nature of the universe is known.

[1] *Siris*, § 297.   [2] Ibid., § 252.

We may now properly turn from Berkeley's criticism of science and its pretensions to truth to a consideration of his own positive metaphysical views, based as they are on his view of the nature of spirit and our apprehension of it. Here we may admit at once that we shall find on every hand an absence of that logical discipline and careful attention to detail which characterizes his criticism of the views of the Materialists or Minute Philosophers. Convinced as he was, first and always, that the essence of Reality was spiritual, and that it was through our experience of spirit, and this alone, that the secrets of the universe could be solved, Berkeley looked far less rigorously for a satisfactory logical justification of his view; and he made very little attempt at a careful exposition of the evidence on which his beliefs rest. Attending as he did far more to the attacking of the enemy, his relatively feeble defence of his positive metaphysical faith fell an easy victim to the ruthless logic of Hume. It is not here that Berkeley as philosopher is to be seen at his best, however much we may admire the energy and clarity of style of Berkeley the dogmatic preacher. It is rather on his carrying of the war into the enemy's country, and wrestling with mathematician, physicist, and psychologist on their own ground that his fame as a philosopher securely rests. By the same token there will be found to be little if any real development in his spiritualism: the teaching of the *Siris* is in this respect different only in negligible details from that of the *Principles* and *Dialogues*.

We have already seen in our consideration of the *Principles* that on Berkeley's view the universe depends for its reality on God. The physical world has no existence except in the sensations which God presents to us. It was unnecessary for God to make a physical world, since

He could as easily give us the experiences which we have without creating any such thing. For the benefit of man God ordains that sensuous experience shall be orderly; in order that we may live a safe and convenient life He ordains that our presentations shall conform in general to certain rules which we call laws of nature. We must beware of thinking of these laws as indicating any causality in nature. The only cause is God, who causes our presentations, and arranges that the appearance of one may be a sign to us of the appearance of another, for our convenience of living. This misleads the unwary into thinking that the representations or objects cause one another. But on analysis it is clear, Berkeley urges, that we have no experience of any such natural causation; all that we directly experience is the uniform succession of our presentations. The relation between cause and effect is indeed arbitrary; they are connected by no necessary tie; the connexion depends on God's good pleasure alone, and while He commonly preserves the orderliness of nature for our benefit, yet His freedom is in no way limited. In his later philosophy, Berkeley emphasizes less and less the dominance of the consideration of man's interest, and insists more and more on the dependence of the world on a sublime God, whose will is ultimately quite arbitrary and free, and whose ways are inscrutable and beyond our understanding. It has been well said that while in the *Dialogues* Berkeley's universe is really anthropocentric, God sustaining it for man's benefit, in the metaphysical parts of *Siris* man and his interests are entirely subordinate to God.[1]

The position of finite selves in Berkeley's metaphysic is not quite clear. Spirit of course is real: it is indeed the

[1] G. A. Johnston, *The Development of Berkeley's Philosophy*, p. 252.

only reality, being the only active thing in the universe. Finite spirits show their activity by willing, operating in the world and causing their own representations in imagination. But, since they can create neither selves nor presentations to sense, their activity is inferior to God's; and as percipient of God's presentations they are really passive. They are thus wholly dependent for their activity and reality on God—though in a different sense from that in which the physical world is dependent on God, in that they enjoy a certain measure of real freedom and activity in the moral life.

Now it is clear that in support of this bold and simple metaphysic Berkeley must hold a special theory in regard to our knowledge of spirit. He has sought to prove that scientific explanations of the nature of the universe really explain nothing. He must now show that his own account gives the true explanation, and he must make clear to us on what evidence his own account is based. How does he know that the only reality in the world is spirit? How can he be sure indeed that there is such a thing as spirit at all? He asserts that his spiritualistic theory can explain the phenomenon of the physical world, while the materialistic hypothesis fails. But such a view requires proof, and we must attempt to determine how far Berkeley gives any such proof, bearing in mind that the verdict of history is that his arguments fell an easy victim to Hume.

Spirits are not to be known, he says in the *Principles*, in the same manner as senseless inactive objects, or by way of *idea*. Spirits and ideas are things wholly different; 'to know a spirit as we do a triangle seems as absurd as if we should hope to *see a sound*'.[1] Clearly I cannot have an idea of spirit, though I may be said to have a 'notion of *my*

[1] *Principles*, § 142.

mind, and its acts about ideas, inasmuch as I know or understand what is meant by these words'.[1] Beyond this Berkeley does not go, though he seems to have recognized that more was required of him, since he promised a Second Part of the *Principles* to deal with the subject fully. He seems generally to assume in his writings that I have knowledge, immediate and infallible, of my mind and its own states; that nothing happens in my mind of which I am unaware, or such that I misapprehend or even incompletely apprehend it. However, he never really goes into the subject at all adequately, and he never attempts to meet the obvious objections.

As regards our knowledge of other finite spirits Berkeley's view is not very clear. It is plain, he says, that we cannot know the existence of other spirits immediately, as we know our own, but only 'by their operations, or the ideas by them excited in us.'[2] By this he seems to mean simply that when we have experience through the senses of operations in the physical world like those which we are aware of producing ourselves, we conclude that they are the work of other spirits. In any case, our particular knowledge of other finite spirits is mediated by sensuous experience: it is not direct and immediate like that of ourselves, and therefore cannot serve, on Berkeley's view, to support a true metaphysic.

The existence of God, he says, is far more evidently perceived than the existence of other men, because the effects of nature which are His handiwork are infinitely more numerous and considerable than those ascribed to human agents. He it is indeed who maintains that intercourse between spirits whereby they are able to perceive

[1] *Principles*, § 142. This sentence was introduced in the second edition.   [2] Ibid, § 145.

the existence of each other. God and His goodness are seen everywhere by 'the eye of the mind'; it is plain that nothing can be more evident to any one that is capable of the least reflection than the existence of God. Yet even here, when pressed, Berkeley would have to admit at the last that on his own showing my knowledge of God is not direct and immediate like my knowledge of myself.

It is clear that Berkeley's views about our apprehension of spirit are a mass of half-articulated dogma. Even the dogma is only half-hearted, for while Berkeley seems bravely to assume that spiritual causation and spiritual activity generally are wholly intelligible, as contrasted with matter, he knows, and admits, that the ways of God, who is pure spirit, are unknowable by us. He must have learnt too from his own introspective researches that the doctrine that we know immediately and exactly all that goes on in our own minds is not without its difficulties; and even if this be granted, it does not carry with it similar conclusions about our knowledge of other spirits and of God. We know that he must have considered the matter, however, with some degree of fairness and impartiality, for clearly at one time he was a sceptic about the existence of individual minds or spirits.[1] Moreover, there is one passage in the *Dialogues* where he seeks dispassionately to argue for the existence of spiritual substance, and he even anticipates the point of Hume's criticism. But his defence is soon seen to be but impotent beating of the air, and to have behind it no careful or detailed analysis comparable to that which he gave to the workings of scientific method.

To come to the conclusion of the whole matter: Berkeley is always, first and last, convinced that the essence of

[1] *Commonplace Book* (Oxford Edition of Berkeley's *Works* i. 27, 31, 38, etc.)

reality is spiritual, and that its true nature is apprehended by us in and through our insight into the activities of spirit. He seeks to discredit rationalism and materialism by showing that science deals only with the sensible; this being mind-dependent, its full apprehension must also ultimately be dependent upon the apprehension of mind or spirit, which he thought to be the work of philosophy and theology; at any rate the possibility of such knowledge is essentially closed to physical science by the fact that its fundamental concepts are derived from the senses. At first, in the *Principles*, he expresses this view that science deals with the sensible so forcibly and crudely that he becomes involved in the view that the *esse* of the scientific mind is *percipere*, that knowing is perceiving. Gradually, under the influence of his close and valuable investigations of the method of science, and also perhaps of his reading of Plato and Aristotle, he recognizes that this cannot be maintained, since it is clear that 'the principles of science are neither objects of sense nor imagination'.[1] He therefore ultimately admits that even scientific knowledge depends on notions, that is, on our apprehension of mind, which is not derived from the senses. With this admission he really abandons empiricism, and is left without any epistemological justification for his view that science cannot apprehend the true nature of reality, since it is now recognized to work, like philosophy and theology, with conceptions which have their origin in our immediate knowledge of spirit, and about objects which cannot be understood by sense, their *esse* being, not to be perceived by man, but to work together for good and to be manifestations of God's inscrutable purposes. Berkeley's followers were right in recognizing that the early

[1] *Siris*, § 264.

Berkeley of the *Principles* and *Dialogues* is the consistent Berkeley, but they did not see that he has himself shown, by a rigorous analysis, that his own view cannot be maintained.

3. *Moral Theory.*

Berkeley never published any systematic account of his ethical views, though it is certain that at one time he meant to do so. In early days he expected his New Principle to solve moral problems as well as others, and he proposed to demonstrate this in the Second Part of the *Principles of Human Knowledge*, which never saw the light. It seems fair to conclude, however, from sufficient material scattered up and down Berkeley's writings, that he could never have occupied a place of first-class importance in the history of British moral theory. In the case of Ethics the main stream of speculative thought does not pass through Locke as it did in regard to problems of knowledge; and Berkeley, whose speculations are here as elsewhere in close relation to those of Locke, is left in a backwater.[1]

Taking his cue from Locke, Berkeley seems to have felt at first that the mathematical demonstration of ethics was a task lying ready to his hand. Morals, he says, is 'mixt mathematics'.[2] On his own view of mathematics, this is quite consistent with his other view that ethics is a practical science, concerned with actual conduct, its aim being 'the good cause of the world'. Ethics, indeed, is not, he says, concerned with ideas at all; as we can neither perceive nor imagine virtue or vice in abstraction from concrete particular actions which are virtuous or vicious, moral theory

[1] Cf. G. A. Johnston, *Development of Berkeley's Philosophy*, p. 317.
[2] *Commonplace Book*. (Oxford Edition of Berkeley's *Works*, i. 46.)

cannot be concerned with our perceptions or imaginations. Demonstration in morals can only deal with words or signs; we need only to 'make a dictionary of words, and see which included which'.[1] In all this Berkeley is evidently applying wholesale to morals his general theory of reasoning, derived from his examination of mathematics. He seems neither to be showing, nor even to claim to be showing, any specifically moral insight.

In any case, he seems quite early to have abandoned the idea of approximating moral inquiry to the mathematical. At any rate there is no reference later than the *Principles* to a possible mathematical science of ethics. His ethical views in *Passive Obedience* and in *Alciphron* are concerned with the discussion of entirely different matters. Like Kant, though for different reasons, Berkeley is convinced that universal rules are essential to the moral life. He criticizes strongly the view that a man should calculate in each individual case what will be for the greatest general good. In the first place, he says, consequences cannot be calculated, and even if they could the process would take far too long to afford a method of practical living. In the second place, no *system* of ethics would be possible on this view; each man would have his own private opinion, moral appraisement would be impossible, and all effective distinction between good and evil would be lost. From these considerations Berkeley rather easily concludes that there must be rigid laws in morality, to which no exception can be allowed.

These laws, he says, are rational and natural; they are agreeable to, and grow from, the 'most excellent and peculiar part of human nature'.[2] They are eternal laws

[1] *Commonplace Book* (Oxford Edition of Berkeley's *Works*, i. 39)
[2] *Alciphron*, First Dialogue, § 14.

of nature and of reason, because they naturally and necessarily result from the nature of things; and they are based on three fundamental postulates—God, freedom, and immortality—which are themselves ultimate and rational. The moral laws are also divine; they are the arbitrary, but not capricious, volitions of God, so determined by Him as to form together a system of rules, which will necessarily promote the true welfare of mankind.

Thus side by side with his divine authoritarianism, Berkeley also finds a place for his so-called 'Utilitarianism'. The ultimate criterion of good and evil, he thinks, is tendency to promote or thwart happiness; and it is a natural principle that we consider things in the light of our own happiness. As to the meaning of happiness, Berkeley in his early days, as we should expect, declares roundly that sensuous pleasure is the *summum bonum*, though he recognizes that intelligence is required to ensure the maximum of sensuous pleasure and the minimum of sensuous pain. Later on, in the *Alciphron*, he maintains that sensuous pleasure is natural only to brutes. Reason is the highest and most characteristic element in human nature, and only rational pleasures are in the strict sense natural to man. Reason also shows us that the *summum bonum* is not mere temporal happiness. Eternal happiness can be guaranteed only by God. Hence rational self-love lays it down that in order to secure the *summum bonum* we must act always in accordance with the will of God. This fortunately solves the problem of egoism and altruism, since God has laid down that we shall secure the highest good to ourselves by doing good to others.

Berkeley's attitude to contemporary writers on moral subjects is highly unsatisfactory. In the *Alciphron* he criticizes the views of Mandeville and Shaftesbury. In the

Letter to Dion it has been easily shown by Mandeville himself that Berkeley fundamentally misrepresents his view in a way which may even be disingenuous; and he seems quite incapable of understanding Shaftesbury's point of view at all. Of his great contemporary, Butler, whose view is so similar to Berkeley's except in that its peculiar excellence—its psychological insight into the practical moral life—is almost entirely absent from Berkeley's ethical writings, there is no mention whatever in any of his works.

From this short summary it is evident enough that Berkeley's greatness as a philosopher does not betray itself in the results of his moral inquiry. Here his weakness of accepting and propounding authoritarian views of his own, without any readiness to turn his great critical acumen upon himself, is more marked than ever. He makes no attempt to choose finally between the two views which are to be found in solution in his writings; the first and predominant view being that God is the ultimate reality, and to do His will is the moral life—in which event happiness has nothing to do with it; the second, that good and bad are determined by the calculation of happiness, God being, in this connexion, merely part of the mechanism which ensures that the sum will come out right. He was not sufficiently clear in his own mind to stand out either as a thoroughgoing authoritarian, or as the first Utilitarian. Nor did he show on the other hand, in this part of his thinking, the combined honesty and insight to see steadily and with unerring vision the essential and inescapable problem of morals, which it is the glory of Butler to have stated once for all in the famous words—'Let it be allowed, though virtue or moral rectitude does indeed consist in affection to and pursuit of what is right and good, as such;

yet, that when we sit down in a cool hour, we can neither justify to ourselves this or any other pursuit, till we are convinced that it will be for our happiness, or at least not contrary to it'.[1]

The truth is that in all his philosophy Berkeley started with an ill-grounded enthusiasm, and was forced to come to a compromise in later years. In the case of his empiricist thesis in regard to the nature of scientific knowledge, he held on long enough, and accomplished sufficient brilliant analysis in support of his early view, to make a contribution of permanent value. This alone rightly ensures him a place as one of the great philosophers.

[1] Butler's *Sermons* (Oxford Edition, p. 173)

HUME

1. *Life.*

DAVID HUME was born in Edinburgh on 26 April 1711. His parents, both of whom came of good Scottish families, owned a small estate, called Ninewells, in Berwickshire on the banks of the Whiteadder, a few miles from the Border. His father died when he was an infant, and his mother, as Hume himself tells us, 'though young and handsome, devoted herself to the rearing and education of her children'. Little is known of Hume's schooling: he probably entered the Greek class at the University of Edinburgh in 1723, but he did not graduate. At the age of seventeen his family tried to make him a lawyer, but this was not a success. Six years later he tried commerce, with the same result.

In 1735 he went to France with a view to prosecuting his studies in a country retreat. 'I resolved', he tells us, 'to make a very rigid frugality supply my deficiency of fortune, to maintain unimpaired my independency, and to regard every object as contemptible except the improvement of my talents in literature.' He had been collecting materials for his work for some years previously in Scotland, and he now appears to have settled down at La Flèche to write his *Treatise of Human Nature*, of which Books I and II appeared in 1739, and Book III in 1740. The work was reviewed appreciatively in the *History of the Works of the Learned* for November 1739, but Hume seems to have been bitterly dissatisfied with its reception. Looking back on this time in later years he said: 'Never literary attempt was more unfortunate; ... it fell deadborn from the press without reaching such a distinction as even to excite a murmur among the zealots.'

In this same year 1740 began Hume's lifelong friendship

with Adam Smith, to whom he sent a copy of the *Treatise*.
In 1741 and 1742 he published anonymously two volumes
of *Essays Moral and Political*, the immediate success of
which was a great comfort to him. Two years later his
friends tried to secure for him the Chair of Ethics and
Pneumatic Philosophy at the University of Edinburgh, but
the council rejected him on the ground of atheism. In
1746 and 1748 he acted as secretary to General St. Clair
on missions abroad, and seems to have acquitted himself
with credit. He returned to London in 1749, and for the
next two years he was engaged in writing *The Dialogues
on Natural Religion* (which were not published until after
his death), the *Inquiry concerning the Principles of Morals*
(published in 1751), and the *Political Discourses* (published
in 1752). The latter had a great and immediate success.
They were translated into French in 1753, and conferred
on Hume a European reputation.

By this time Hume had a moderate income, partly owing
to his frugal habits, and he seems to have recognized
himself as 'one of the happy and fortunate'. In 1752, the
Faculty of Advocates in Edinburgh elected him their
librarian, but not without opposition. Two years later he
published the first volume of the *History of Great Britain*,
containing the reign of James I and Charles I: its sale was
large at first, but it was abused by all parties—by 'English,
Scotch and Irish, Whig and Tory, Churchman and
Sectary, Freethinker and Religionist, Patriot and Courtier,
The second volume, published in 1756, met with a better
reception. In 1757 appeared the *Natural History of Religion*, and during the next two years Hume was in London
writing the *History of England under the House of Tudor*,
the appearance of which also, according to him, raised a
considerable clamour.

From 1763 to 1769 Hume emerged from his customary seclusion to play a part in public life. In 1763 he went to France as secretary to the ambassador, Lord Hertford: here, where his fame was greater than in England, and where he seems to have been greatly favoured and liked in society, Hume was very happy. He returned to London in 1776 with Rousseau, whom he had befriended. A few months later there occurred between them one of the most famous quarrels and reconciliations ever known between men of letters. In 1767 Hume undertook the duties of an Under-secretary of State for two years. In 1769 he retired, 'very opulent', to Edinburgh, where he built himself a house in what came to be called St. David's Street. Here he lived for some years with his sister, in great content, his house the centre of the accomplished society which then distinguished Edinburgh. In 1775 his health began to fail, and, learning that his disease was mortal, he wrote *My Own Life*, a simple dignified narrative ending with a probably fair appreciation of his own character. He died in Edinburgh on 25 August 1776.

The story of Hume's life, consisting, as it does, chiefly of a list of publications, is not exciting; and the same is true of his character. His only characteristic on the grand scale, which was perhaps also his only vice, was his insatiable appetite for literary fame. Apart from this, he was evidently, as he represents himself, an attractive genial person—'a man of mild dispositions, of command of temper, of an open, social and cheerful humour, capable of attachment, but little susceptible of enmity'. As he says, even his love of literary fame never seriously soured his temper; unless an exception must be made in view of his violently expressed hatred of the English nation, who, as he thought, never properly appreciated his true worth. In spite of the advanced and unpopular nature of his opinions he never found reason to complain of calumny. Perhaps there is to be found in this the greatest tribute to his personal character. At any rate, he tells us with justifiable pride—'Though I wantonly exposed myself to the rage of both civil and religious factions, they seemed to be disarmed in my behalf of their wonted fury.' Throughout his life, those who knew him well loved him, and the dignified resignation with which he bore his last long and painful illness may rightly command the respect of all men.

2. *Theory of Knowledge.*

As is shown by the sub-title of the *Treatise of Human Nature*, Hume's main interest in his approach to his philosophical inquiry was a rationalistic one. His aim was to apply the methods of physical science to human nature and thus to build a Science of Man. This he thought must obviously be the most basic of all sciences. Only when founded on such a basis could any system of knowledge be securely built. The reading of literature and the conversation of fellow-men, he says, reveal the most divergent opinions on all subjects: the most curious and paradoxical of theories, if put forward with sufficient art, will always be believed by some one. This is because no one has yet used the powerful instrument of modern scientific discipline to go to the root of the matter—that is, to study by observation, diligently and without preconceived theories, the nature and powers of man. The time has now come to do this. And Hume, while he does not expect wholly to succeed where so many men of genius have failed, offers his own attempt to apply scientific method to the solution of the fundamental problems of philosophy.

It is of the greatest importance to remember when

reading Hume that he did not approach this task with any
leaning toward scepticism. He wrote in an age when men
entertained the greatest possible hopes of science; when
they did not hesitate to believe that all the problems of
the universe would soon be solved by the unaided power
of disciplined reason. And in this respect Hume was a true
child of his age. When he found that an unbounded faith
in science was not, as far as he could see, justified, he was
horror-stricken: and he was ready to believe that he must
have made some mistake in his inquiry, though diligent
search failed to reveal that mistake. Moreover, paradoxical
as it may seem, it was his extreme faith in reason which
was responsible for his scepticism. His philosophical
scepticism is but the obverse of an extremely confident
and dogmatic psychology. He showed such enthusiasm
in applying the method of experimental science to psychology that he made the most extravagant claims in this
regard without even noticing it. He did not ask himself
whether scientific method could properly be applied to the
study of mind: it did not even occur to him to look for
new and special difficulties in applying it. More than this,
we shall see that his scepticism depends not merely on the
assumption that psychology can be an exact science, but
further on the assumption that such a science, true in all
essential principles, had sprung fully armed from his own
brain. For his scepticism depends upon the truth of his
account of the origin and causes of belief in the mind of
man: if this account fails, there remains nothing to support
his sceptical conclusions. Unless he can show that all our
beliefs not only could, but did in all cases, arise in just
the way he asserts, then the conclusion must be that there
is more involved in the birth of knowledge than his psychology has discovered, and that recourse must be had to

further and deeper psychological inquiry. Yet Hume never saw this: he always takes his arguments in this sphere to be as complete and as unquestionable as mathematical proofs.

Hume wrote then as a builder of the Science of Human Nature, and it was as such that he exercised his main influence on his successors. He encouraged in men the hope of the successful extension of scientific progress to human nature itself: thus might come a reasoned, definitive and accurate answer to all problems—religious, moral, social, and political. If the workings of the human mind were to lie open like a book, then there should be no difficulty which could not be overcome: therein would lie the clue to truth by means of the scrutiny of the origins of belief, and a highroad to general happiness by means of the understanding and control of the origins of emotions and of action. Here was a rationalist indeed: the founder, with Butler and Hartley, of that belief in and enthusiasm for the Science of Human Nature which was so important in the philosophy and in the practical politics of the nineteenth century.

It is true that in approaching the problem of knowledge from the psychological side Hume was but following Locke and Berkeley. Both these thinkers were confident of the possibility of a scientific psychology; they both believed that a full rational account of the necessary behaviour of mind could be arrived at by observation of the conscious activities of minds. But the final act of faith in the new science was not required of either of these, as it was required of Hume. Both Locke and Berkeley were satisfied that their psychology justified a belief in human knowledge, and even in physical science. They did not therefore have to choose between their faith in psychology and their common system of beliefs; indeed they were rather strengthened in their faith in the new science because of its supposed capacity to explain and justify both common knowledge and physics. Hume alone was forced to the final choice; and he chose, almost without noticing it, to put complete faith in his own psychology, even at the cost of rejecting any confidence either in his ordinary beliefs or in the discoveries of physical science. This view of the matter is confirmed by the subsequent history of philosophy. One school of thinkers maintained that Hume could only be refuted by refuting his own special psychology; Kant and his followers thought that refutation was only possible by recognizing the incompetence of psychology as such to solve the problems of knowledge. Both schools saw that it was the rationalistic and dogmatic side of Hume which must be attacked.

Hume assumed then that psychology, following the experimental method of physical science, could discover and explain the origins of belief: that it could expose all the action and passion of mind which is relevant to the birth of knowledge in the soul. When he found that all the happenings in the mind which his psychology could detect did not justify a conviction of the certainty of knowledge, he became a sceptic. Subsequent philosophy has shown that the main interest in the study of Hume centres in this question: was Hume's failure to represent knowledge as valid due to the special mistakes of Hume as a psychologist, or was it due to the psychological approach in itself? Are we to say with Kant that the psychologist is necessarily a sceptic, and conclude that the philosopher must in the last resort repudiate psychology and look for another method? Or may we retain our hopes of psychology, and simply look for and avoid

Hume's particular mistakes? In the main line of its development, English philosophy has held to the second alternative.

Hume's method then was psychological. We must now ask, what was psychology to Hume? Hume, like Locke, believed that the most fundamental of all inquiries was the inquiry into the powers of the mind. In this inquiry the object of investigation was the mind itself, and so the mind must be treated as a physical object is treated in physical science.[1] It must be closely observed and its behaviour under varying conditions noted until the laws of its nature are discovered. Thus it was Hume's problem to describe exactly all the contents of the individual mind, and in particular to determine the necessary conditions of the origination and development of conscious experience in the individual mind. The possibility that the mind might have any contents in it prior to conscious experience was not, of course, entertained:[2] it was assumed that in the case of any idea present in the mind, its origin and growth must be capable of being discovered by the observation of that particular mind's conscious experience: it was assumed that no change or development of any idea could occur

[1] In one passage Hume does admit that there is a special difficulty involved in treating the mind in this way. 'When I am at a loss', he says, 'to know the effects of one body upon another in any situation, I need only put them in that situation, and observe what results from it. But should I endeavour to clear up after the same manner any doubt in moral philosophy, by placing myself in the same case with that which I consider, 'tis evident this reflection and premeditation would so disturb the operation of my natural principles, as must render it impossible to form any just conclusion from the phenomenon' (*Treatise*, Introd. *ad fin*). But having looked the difficulty firmly in the face, Hume passes on, simply noting that special care is required.

[2] Cf. Locke's attack on Innate Principles.

except as conditioned by some conscious experience. The assumption may be put crudely like this, and it must be admitted that it looks innocent enough: since knowledge is born in the individual mind, if we watch the behaviour of that individual mind we shall see it being born; and if we watch closely enough we should be able to notice all the conditions which are necessary to that knowledge, and so to knowledge in general. Having thus discovered how knowledge actually comes to be, we shall be able to examine its claims, and accept or reject them. Thus Hume is careful to make sure that he has noticed *all* that is going on in the mind in the case of any given mental process, and his last word to an objector is—rightly, on his own method—to challenge him to look into his own mind to see if he can find present any element which his own inquiry has missed.

The development and structure of Hume's work follow directly and necessarily from the fundamental principle of his method. First, he gives a careful account of the contents of mind, attempting to describe exactly all the elements that can be discovered in conscious experience. Secondly, he examines those judgements which are grounded in the 'formal elements of experience', space and time. In the third part he analyses the relation of cause and effect, the principle that underlies real connexions between the elements of experience. And finally he considers his results, attempting to determine the ultimate significance of experience.

First of all then it is necessary to determine the contents of the mind, the elemental stuff (so Hume thinks of it) of which our highly complex experience is made. If we look into our own minds, he says, we find that all the contents resolve themselves into two distinct kinds—*impressions* and *ideas*. The difference between these consists in the degrees of force and liveliness with which they strike upon the mind. Every one of himself will readily perceive the difference between feeling and thinking: the impressions which we feel when the object is present to us are far clearer and more lively than the ideas which we have when we remember our experience of the object in its absence. It is true that in sleep, in a fever, in madness, or in any very violent emotions of soul, our ideas may approach to our impressions; as on the other hand it sometimes happens that our impressions are so faint and low that we cannot distinguish them from our ideas. But notwithstanding, he says, impressions and ideas are in general so very different that no one will scruple to rank them under distinct heads.[1]

Hume notices that he is using the words *impression* and *idea* in a sense different from what is usual; but he considers that he is rather restoring the word idea to its original sense, from which Locke had perverted it by making it stand for all our perceptions. He also notices an ambiguity in the word impression, which he tries to remove: 'By the term of impression I would not be understood to express the manner in which our lively perceptions are produced in the soul, but merely the perceptions themselves.'[2] These words are not very clear: but it seems that Hume is confusedly distinguishing between the act of perceiving and that which is perceived—that is, for instance, between the hearing and the noise heard, the seeing and the colour

[1] After this he seems to take it for granted that there is no serious difficulty in distinguishing between perception and memory or imagination. He speaks as if we know at once in the act of awareness. The difficulty of distinguishing between memory and imagination he deals with later.

[2] *Treatise*, I. i, § 1, foot-note.

seen; and that he is asserting that, granting this distinction, that which is perceived is an impression. It appears that he is without hesitation or criticism following Locke in his general view that what we perceive is a mental image, while offering his distinction of two kinds of mental image, impressions and ideas, as a refinement on Locke's view.

It is essential to Hume to maintain that this analysis of the contents of the mind is exhaustive; that is, that there is nothing to be found in the mind which is not either an impression or an idea. Both, he notices, may be either simple or complex: but there is nothing of which the mind can be aware that does not fall under one class or the other. To meet any objection to his view, Hume simply challenges the objector to look into his own mind and find there anything which is neither an impression nor an idea.

Impressions and ideas then differ from one another in respect of their degrees of force and vivacity; but it is to be noticed, says Hume, that in every other particular they are alike. Every idea seems to be in a manner the reflection of an impression, so that 'all the perceptions of the mind are double, and appear both as impressions and ideas'; and these always appear to correspond to each other.[1] It is plain that in speaking of ideas and impressions, Hume is here thinking of the relation of memory, or imagination, and original perception; both he regards as awareness of mental images, differing in respect of their force and vivacity. This becomes clearer in the passage which follows, where he seeks to prove that to every idea there is a corresponding impression. Upon a more accurate survey he says, it appears that many of our complex ideas never had impressions corresponding to them, and that many of our complex impressions never are exactly copied in ideas.

[1] *Treatise*, I. i, § I.

'I can imagine to myself such a city as the *New Jerusalem*, whose pavement is gold and walls are rubies, tho' I never saw any such. I have seen *Paris*; but shall I affirm I can form such an idea of that city, as will perfectly represent all its streets and houses in their real and just proportions?'[1] Having made this point about complex ideas and impressions, that while they commonly correspond to one another, yet they do not universally do so, Hume allows them to pass out of his discussion. He is primarily concerned to argue that simple impressions and ideas necessarily and universally correspond.

A word must be said, however, about this passage. Here it is quite clear that Hume is speaking of ideas as mental images, in this case the images of the New Jerusalem and of Paris: but it is to be presumed that these images only differ in complexity from the mental images which are simple ideas. He speaks here, too, as if there were single impressions corresponding to the most complicated perceptions. He says he has *seen* Paris; that is, that he was aware of a complex impression of Paris. In other words he is assuming here that the imagination plays no part in any perception whatever, a view which is probably not his ordinary view: he speaks as if Paris could be seen in the same sense as colour is seen or a noise is heard, the perception in each case being a simple awareness of an impression. Too much importance, however, should not be attached to this difficulty, since Hume's main argument can be stated and his conclusions drawn without any reference to complex impressions. But it may be noticed that Hume, who is ordinarily so acute a critic, often fails to apply his acuteness to the criticism of his own psychology. Furthermore, if he had forced himself definitely to

[1] Ibid.

make up his mind whether there are or are not such things as complex impressions, he might at least have changed his theory of perception; though, as we shall see, it is unlikely that his general theory of knowledge would have been essentially different.

Be that as it may, Hume does insist that simple ideas and impressions always exactly and necessarily correspond, and for argument challenges the reader to find a simple impression that has not a corresponding idea, or a simple idea that has not a corresponding impression. This constant conjunction of ideas and impressions, he urges, cannot arise from chance; it clearly proves, in accordance with the rules of procedure of Newtonian science, the dependence of the one upon the other. To determine on which side this dependence lies, we have only to consider the order of their first appearance; here we find by constant experience that the simple impressions always precede the corresponding ideas. This priority proves that our impressions are the causes of our ideas, not our ideas of our impressions. This is further confirmed by the fact that where, owing to deficiencies in or absence of organs, we have not the impressions, we never have the corresponding ideas. Hume grants indeed the existence of one contradictory phenomenon, which may prove, he says, that it is not absolutely impossible for ideas to go before their corresponding impressions. If all the different shades of a colour, except one, be placed before a man who has sight, he will be conscious of the blank, and can by his imagination supply the deficiency. But Hume easily dismisses this contrary instance; it is 'so particular and singular, that 'tis scarce worth our observing, and does not merit that, for it alone, we should alter our general maxim'.[1] So

[1] *Treatise*, I. i, § I. This somewhat cavalier treatment of con-

he regards himself as having established the general proposition, 'that all our simple ideas in their first appearance are deriv'd from simple impressions, which are correspondent to them, and which they exactly represent'.[1]

This principle must not be despised because of the simplicity of its appearance. The question involved is indeed the same, Hume says, as one which 'has made so much noise in other terms';[2] the question, that is, whether there are *innate ideas*, or whether all our ideas proceed from sensation and reflection. This problem was, of course, raised by Locke, who thought he had settled it, first by his attack on innate principles, and secondly by his own constructive account on empirical principles of the process by which knowledge is born. Hume speaks as if he thought that Locke's position was sound, though ambiguously stated; but that his own more careful statement had made the matter clear once and for all. He is certainly right, however, in pointing out that this principle, which looks so innocent, is of far-reaching importance from his own point of view; for having laid it down, he proceeds to argue that it follows that where there can be found in experience no impression, there can be in the mind no corresponding idea, in spite of all appearances to the contrary. Moreover, as we shall see, it is by the use of this argument that he develops his most striking conclusions.

Having now determined the contents of the mind, Hume proposes to examine what *happens* to these contents within

trary instances, which appears to us so alien from the spirit of science, is not peculiar to Hume: instances of a similar attitude to exceptional cases will readily be recalled in the works of Adam Smith and Ricardo, who first applied the method of physical science to economic theory.   [1] Ibid.   [2] Ibid.

the mind; and he turns to examine those mental operations, which are commonly included under the general name of *thinking*. He approaches this inquiry by way of a distinction between ideas of imagination and ideas of memory. An impression which has been present in the mind, he says, may reappear in two different ways—either as an idea of memory or as an idea of imagination. Ideas of memory are much more lively and strong than those of the imagination. There is also a further difference; while neither can appear in the mind unless the impressions have gone before to prepare the way, the imagination is not tied down in respect of the order and form of the original impressions, while the memory is 'in a manner' so tied, without any power of variation. This liberty which the imagination has to transpose and change the order and form of its ideas is shown by the fables of winged horses, fiery dragons, and monstrous giants. Wherever the imagination perceives a difference among ideas, Hume says, it can easily produce a separation, and having separated can recombine in a different order.

Thus it seems at first sight that nothing could be more free and unaccountable than the operations of the imagination. But it is easily seen that this is not really so. Analysis reveals that the imagination is in fact guided by certain 'universal principles, which render it, in some measure, uniform with itself in all times and places'.[1] If ideas were entirely loose and unconnected, chance alone would join them; and there would be no regularity observable in their conjunction. But in fact the same simple ideas are constantly falling into the same complex ones in the same way. This must clearly be due, Hume says, to 'some bond of union, some associating quality, by which one idea

[1] *Treatise*, I. i, § 4.

naturally introduces another'.[1] This uniting principle is not an inseparable connexion; the mind is not so limited by it, that without it it cannot join two ideas. It is to be regarded rather as 'a gentle force, which commonly prevails, and is the cause why, among other things, languages so nearly correspond to each other, nature in a manner pointing out to every one those simple ideas, which are most proper to be united in a complex one'.[2]

This association of ideas, Hume continues, seems to be based on certain qualities in the ideas associated. He does not mean that the possibility of association depends upon *the apprehension by the mind* of certain qualities in the ideas. This is not his point. He is not attempting to explain *how* association arises. He never argues, as Kant does, that association itself would never be possible without an active mind, since he sees no empirical evidence to assure him of this. He just accepts association as an observed fact, and simply asks himself what are the particular principles of this association as observed; what it is, in other words, that determines that a particular tune should be associated in my mind with a particular person, rather than with another person, or indeed with a place, a picture, or a scent. His answer is that wherever there is association, there will always be found as a matter of fact certain qualities in the ideas. He is carefully following the strict Newtonian method, attempting to assert nothing but what he observes. Where there are certain qualities in the ideas, there the ideas are found to be associated; that is all that can be said. Whether or not Hume's analysis is complete, at least he is strict in the application of his method.

The qualities concerned, he says, are three in number:

[1] Ibid.   [2] Ibid

resemblance, contiguity in time or place, and cause and effect. It is plain that our imagination runs easily from one idea to another that resembles it. It is also evident that as the senses in changing their objects take them as they lie contiguous to each other, the imagination must by long custom acquire the same method of thinking. With regard to cause and effect, which would perhaps seem to present difficulties when regarded as a quality of the idea, Hume simply refers the reader forward; we shall have occasion afterwards, he says, to examine it to the bottom, and therefore shall not at present insist upon it.

The principle of the association of ideas Hume compares to the principle of universal attraction in physics. The variety of its manifestations is as manifold, he says, and *the causes and mode of its operation as unknown*. Its existence must be accepted on the evidence of observation. It will perhaps be well to quote Hume's own words. 'Here is a kind of ATTRACTION, which in the mental world will be found to have as extraordinary effects as in the natural, and to show itself in as many and as various forms. Its effects are everywhere conspicuous: but as to its causes, they are mostly unknown, and must be resolved into *original* qualities of human nature, which I pretend not to explain. Nothing is more requisite for a true philosopher, than to restrain the intemperate desire of searching into causes.'[1] Hume is building a science of the human mind, and his first principle he regards as just as well, and just as badly, founded as the first principle of physics—a principle, that is, which the impartial observer is forced to recognize as actually operative in nature, though it is beyond his powers to apprehend *how* it operates.

So far Hume has been simply noticing these principles

[1] *Treatise*, I. i, § 4.

of association as being actual principles which in fact seem to underlie operations of the imagination. He now goes on to attempt to show that these principles underlie *all* connexions of ideas in the mind; that there are no mental operations whatever which cannot be adequately explained on these principles, since even the disciplined reasoning of science reveals itself on analysis to be nothing more nor less than association of ideas.

The operations of thought Hume treats as falling under three heads: the apprehension of *relations*, of *modes*, and of *substances*. All these are apprehended by thought, not by perception: their apprehension involves not merely the reception of impressions, but certain mental operations stimulated by the reception of impressions. The whole interest and nerve of this part of Hume's argument turns on his examination of our apprehension of relations, and in particular on his careful and lengthy discussion of the apprehension of the relation of cause and effect. This part of Hume's analysis has always been regarded as the central point of his teaching. It is therefore necessary to give special attention to the examination of it; for here lies the stronghold of his scepticism. It has indeed been commonly said that the problem for subsequent philosophy has been and is to defend the causal principle against Hume's attack.

He first seeks to show—and this, as we shall see, is essential to his general argument—that the causal principle is the basic principle upon which the validity of all knowledge depends. If we have not the capacity, he says, to apprehend causal processes, then we can have no knowledge. Unless Hume can prove this point, his attack on the causal principle itself is of very minor importance; if the causal principle is only one principle among many, as Kant seems to have thought, then his attack on it can only invalidate one of many principles, and certainly cannot support a general scepticism. We must first, then, examine the way by which Hume came to this doctrine; though we may bear in mind that nearly all his English commentators and critics have agreed in commending him for being the first to lay down this principle unequivocally; that is to say, most of these philosophers have agreed with Hume in his teaching that the causal principle is the one basic principle of all thought.

He distinguishes seven kinds of relations, which he divides into two classes: first, resemblance, contrariety, degrees in any quality, and proportions in quantity or number; secondly, identity, relations of time and place, and cause and effect. About the first class of relations Hume has very little to say, and that little very obscure. He clearly thinks that these relations are from his point of view of very little importance, at any rate in view of the observations which he has to make about the second class. The relations of the first class he says 'depend entirely on the ideas',[1] and they can be the objects of knowledge and certainty. Resemblance, contrariety, and degrees of quality are apprehended immediately by intuition; proportions in quantity or number, it is true, require reasoning for their apprehension, but this reasoning, depending entirely on the ideas, is abstract and exact. Thus within this sphere Hume explicitly allows for certain and exact knowledge by means of intuition and abstract reasoning.[2]

[1] *Treatise*, I. iii, § I.

[2] Hume's statements in regard to our knowledge of quantity and number are inexact and confused. In general, of course, it is the consideration of mathematical science which brings him face to face with his gravest difficulties, and exposes most clearly the

So far this seems to conflict with his general view that the causal principle is the basic principle of all reasoning; but it will be seen in the sequel that this contradiction is to some extent corrected, and is in any case not important, since on Hume's view the apprehension of these relations cannot properly be dignified by the name of knowledge, as it concerns only ideas and is not 'knowledge of real existences'.

Turning to the second class of relations, Hume says these are 'such as may be changed without any change in the ideas';[1] hence, since they do not 'depend on the ideas alone', they cannot be apprehended by intuition or by abstract reasoning. Of these we receive information from experience: nor can they be the objects of knowledge and certainty. In this class, also, two of the relations can be apprehended without any need of reasoning. When both the objects, he says, are present to the senses along with inadequacy of his basic principles. Kant was essentially right in urging that had he closely thought out these difficulties he must have modified his position. In his treatment Hume separates geometry from arithmetic and algebra. His view seems to be that all geometrical propositions are derived from observation, whether ideal or actual, and that therefore their supposed universality and exactness differ only in degree from 'the loose judgments of the senses and imagination'. Ideas of perfect lines, figures, and surfaces have according to him no existence, since there are no corresponding impressions. He gives no specific account of the way in which geometrical knowledge, such as it is, is derived from impressions. As regards number, he simply asserts, in defiance of his general view, that we have absolutely exact arithmetical propositions; but he offers no explanation as to how on his own theory this can be so.

For a careful discussion of Hume's view of mathematics see Adamson's article in the *Encyclopaedia Britannica* (ninth ed. xii. 353).

[1] *Treatise*, I. iii, § I.

the relation, our apprehension is rather by perception than by reasoning, since there is not involved any activity (properly speaking), that is, no exercise of thought, but a 'mere passive admission of the impressions thro' the organs of sensation'.[1] In none of these cases 'can the mind go beyond what is immediately present to the senses, either to discover the real existence or the relations of objects'.[2] This can only be done by means of the causal relation, the manner of apprehension of which we have yet to examine.

There is no doubt that Hume's treatment of the apprehension of these relations is highly unsatisfactory. He speaks as if such apprehension was the unaided work of simple perception: that is to say, he speaks as if 'right and left' or 'distance' are apprehended by perception in the same sense as colour is apprehended by perception—a view to which no follower of Berkeley could seriously adhere.[3] He also speaks as if there were impressions of relations, an assertion which is in flat contradiction with his general view. But the truth seems to be that Hume is giving little attention to his positive account of the apprehension of these relations. He is primarily trying to show that the relation of cause and effect is in an important sense in a class apart from all other relations: that it is, to put it roughly, the only relation which matters from the point of view of knowledge of real existence. His view is that the apprehension of the relations of identity and position in time or place either does not help towards a knowledge of real existences, or, in so far as it does help, is dependent upon the relation of cause and effect, so that this latter relation remains the basic relation of all knowledge. No doubt it would have been more satisfactory if Hume,

[1] *Treatise*, I. iii, § 2.   [2] Ibid.   [3] Cf. *supra*, p. 79.

instead of saying that identity and position in time and place are apprehended by sense, had said that their apprehension depends upon the apprehension of causal relations. In fact Hume does sometimes speak as if this was so, though it is not his official view. But it would have made no difference to his general point—which is that knowledge which goes 'beyond our senses, and informs us of existences and objects, which we do not see or feel',[1] is through and through dependent upon the apprehension of the causal relation.

To sum up, what Hume is really doing is to attempt to show that knowledge depends ultimately on two things, namely, the receiving of simple impressions by the senses, and the connecting of the ideas corresponding to these impressions in accordance with the causal principle. No doubt in his detailed account here Hume sometimes considerably overestimates what is given in sense-perception. But so long as it is agreed, as subsequent philosophers have for the most part agreed, that all other relations are *either* given *or* depend for their apprehension on the causal principle, then Hume is allowed to be right in his main contention here, and the analysis of the causal principle has all the importance which he attributes to it; that is to say, scientific knowledge as a whole stands or falls by it. The only philosophers who have a serious quarrel with Hume on this point are those who hold that there are *other* principles basic to science, whose apprehension carries us beyond what is given in sense and is yet not dependent upon the causal principle.[2]

[1] *Treatise*, I. iii, § 2.
[2] Those who think, for instance, that 'position in time and place' is in some cases apprehended by means of the principle of reciprocity, which, being consistent with reversibility of

In examining our apprehension of the relation of cause
and effect, Hume first seeks a clear understanding of the
idea of 'cause'. It is impossible to understand any idea, he
says, without tracing it to its origin and examining that
primary impression from which it arises. In this case,
there is clearly no one sensible quality by virtue of the
possession of which objects are called 'causes' or 'effects';
that is to say, there is no impression to which the idea of
cause corresponds. How then does this idea come to be?
That is to say, under what conditions does it come into
existence? It would seem that it arises in the mind only
in cases where certain relations are found to exist among
objects. What then are these relations?

Firstly, there is the relation of *contiguity*. Though
distant objects may sometimes appear to be causally related, they are commonly found on examination to be
linked by a chain of causes, all contiguous; even where
these links cannot be discovered they are presumed to
exist. The second relation is that of *priority in time* of the
cause over the effect: this relation, Hume says, is not
universally acknowledged to be necessary to the causal
relation, but is liable to some controversy. But, as he
rightly urges, 'if one cause were co-temporary with its
effect, and this effect with *its* effect, and so on, 'tis plain
there wou'd be no such thing as succession, and all objects
must be co-existent'.[1]

Having discovered these two relations to be necessary
for one thing to be the cause of another, Hume notices that
they alone are not enough. An object may be contiguous

sequence as the causal principle proper is not, is fundamentally
and essentially different from the causal principle, and not
reducible to it. This seems to have been Kant's view.

[1] *Treatise*, I. iii, § 2.

to and prior to another without being considered as its cause. There is *necessary connexion* to be taken into consideration: and this relation is of much greater importance than either of the other two. Yet here the examination of particular instances of causation fails us; we can observe there contiguity and priority, but we can find no other observable relation. But we cannot admit that in this case of necessary connexion we are possessed of an idea not preceded by any corresponding impression, because we have so firmly established the contrary principle. It seems, then, that we are baffled, since further analysis of particular instances is vain.

Hume now resorts to beating about the neighbouring fields, as he puts it: that is, he turns aside to consider two questions, the examination of which he hopes will afford him a hint in his difficulty concerning necessary connexion. First, for what reason do we pronounce it *necessary*, that everything whose existence has a beginning should also have a cause? Secondly, why do we conclude that a certain particular cause must *necessarily* have a certain particular effect, and what is the nature of that *inference* we draw from the one to the other, and of the *belief* we repose in it?

In the first question Hume is asking what are our grounds for asserting the general principle that *whatever begins to exist must have a cause of existence*. With his answer to this question we need not now detain ourselves long. Hume has already urged that the causal relation does not 'depend solely upon ideas'—that is that all the qualities and other relations of the objects concerned may be apprehended by us without our apprehending the causal relation; and that no analysis of the impressions of the objects concerned or of the observable relations between them will reveal to us any causal relation. This being so it must clearly be Hume's view that the general principle of causation cannot be apprehended by intuition or by abstract reasoning. This contention he now proceeds to state and to argue at some length, without raising any new point of importance; and he has no difficulty in showing that the various arguments by which Hobbes, Clarke, and Locke seek to demonstrate the principle all in some form or other assume what they are required to prove. His conclusion is that the principle, since it is clearly in fact operative in our thinking, must have arisen as the result of observation and experience.

The next question, as he says, should naturally be— How does experience give rise in us to the belief that every existence must have a cause? But he prefers to sink this inquiry in the second of the questions which he raised before, viz. Why do we conclude in any particular case that a certain cause must necessarily have a certain effect, and how do we form an inference from one to the other? It will perhaps be found, he says, that the same answer will serve for both questions.[1]

This means that Hume believes that there remains only one way of justifying our belief in the general principle of causation, viz. by showing that in all particular actual cases new existences are found to have causes; that since we never find in experience any new existence which has not a cause, we conclude that this rule holds in all cases, even in cases where so far research has not enabled us to discover what exactly is the cause. This is to say that the possibility of any proof of the general principle must depend on our being convinced of the fact of causation in particular cases, considered on their own merits without any appeal to the

[1] *Treatise*, I. iii, § 3.

general principle. This means that, for Hume's purpose, in the examination of particular cases he must not allow himself to be influenced by the general belief that there must be a cause; he must approach the thing with an open mind, and only believe in the existence of causation if he is convinced of it in particular cases by experiment. After all it is quite conceivable to us that a completely new existence might come into being, undetermined or at least incompletely determined by previous existences.[1] And perhaps we may be forced to admit that, as far as observation and legitimate inference from observation is concerned, this is always the case in our actual experience; that is to say, that always in the case of real change something new springs into existence without any sufficient predetermining cause or reason.

No doubt it may be argued that Hume's point of view requires us to approach experience with an attitude which would never be taken up in practice by any scientist or by any reasonable man. Both in common sense and in scientific method, we should in fact take it for granted that the event had a cause, and we should only expect of our observations and experiments that they should show us whether that cause was A or B or C. Hume agrees that this is so; but his point is that we, in our inquiry into the powers of the human mind, are not entitled to take this line, since we can offer no justification of our assumption. In this he is simply subscribing, without criticism, to the Platonic and Aristotelian doctrine that new knowledge must be derived from previous knowledge: that he who starts from that which he does not know to be true cannot hope to arrive at knowledge in a conclusion. Hume

[1] It would seem that the theories which to-day insist on the category of *emergence* are defending this view.

believes that no good can come of assuming a first principle of whose truth we are not certain. He did his work
so well that he forced Kant to abandon the intransigent
attitude of all previous philosophers on this point, and for
the first time to consider this dogma critically, and finally
to reject it. Since, on Hume's final showing, we cannot
help starting from an assumption whose truth we do not
certainly know, it is of no use to state roundly that no good
can come of such procedure. If this is how our minds
must work, we must examine the matter more patiently,
knowing as we now know, thanks to Hume, that knowledge comes to us by this way or not at all. Thus taught by
Hume the hopelessness of dogmatism, Kant was forced to
try the Critical point of view.

But this is to anticipate a little. We have yet to examine
the account Hume gives of the way in which we come
to believe that a particular event has a particular cause.
Firstly, Hume says, we require to be satisfied of the existence of the cause or of the effect; we can then argue from
the existence of one to the existence of the other. It is not
possible to determine the whole matter by inference alone;
for in that case every link would hang upon another, and
there would not be anything fixed to one end of it, capable
of sustaining the whole; and consequently there would be
no belief or evidence, as is actually the case with all *hypothetical* reasonings. We must then be enabled to start from
an impression which will determine the existence of the
cause or the effect 'beyond all doubt'.

Hume's first task is then to show that we have 'impressions of the memory or senses, beyond which there is no
room for doubt or inquiry'.[1] At first he seems inclined to
discuss the ultimate cause of sense impressions; whether

[1] *Treatise*, I. iii, § 4.

they arise immediately from the object, or are produced by the creative power of the mind, or are derived from the author of our being. But he immediately declares this question to be both unanswerable and impertinent to his inquiry. What is pertinent, he thinks, is that we should be able to distinguish impressions of sense or memory from figments of the imagination. Granted the practical possibility of this distinction, we may fairly leave aside any question as to the origination of the impressions of sense and memory themselves. What matters to us is that impressions of sense and memory are always accompanied in our minds by a *belief* in the existence of the corresponding objects, whereas the ideas of the imagination are not so accompanied. This belief is due, on Hume's view, simply to the superior force and vivacity of those impressions.

We have now satisfied ourselves that we have, and can distinguish, original impressions carrying with them belief in the existence of the objects. We have next to show how we come to make transition from this impression of sense or memory to a separate and distinct idea; that is, how we come *even to think* of some other distant object as connected with the object of which we have the impression. As we have seen, this transition can only be derived from experience; it cannot depend upon intuition or demonstration. Now the nature of experience is this. We remember that in our experience individuals of one species have always attended upon individuals of a certain other species; we remember, for instance, to have seen a flame, and to have felt heat. We call to mind their constant conjunction in all past instances, and without further ceremony we call the one cause and the other effect. In all those instances, of course, from which we learn the conjunction of par-

ticular causes and effects, both the causes and effects were
perceived by the senses, and are remembered; but in all
cases where we reason concerning them, there is only one
perceived or remembered, and the other is supplied in
conformity to our past experience. Thus we come habi-
tually to pass from the impression of sense or memory to a
separate and distinct idea.

Finally, we have still one thing left to explain. We have
shown how it is that we come to entertain the idea of a
connexion between two objects; we have now to explain
how we go beyond this, and come actually to *believe* that
they are in fact so connected. For when we infer from
cause to effect, we move from the impression of the cause
not simply to the idea of the effect, but to a belief in the
existence of the effect. Hume's answer is that here again,
as in the case of the original impression, belief simply
depends on the vivacity of the idea. A short examination
he says will convince any one that this must be so.[1] When
I think of God, when I think of Him as existent, and when
I believe Him to exist, my idea of Him neither increases nor
diminishes. It is clear then that the difference between
belief and incredulity must lie in the manner in which
we conceive the idea, that is, in the force and liveliness of
the idea. What we have to show then in the particular
case under discussion is that we move from the present
impression to a separate and distinct idea which is very
forceful and lively, since it is in this force and liveliness that

---

[1] Strictly speaking, of course, on his own method Hume is not
entitled to argue that anything *must be* so; he should appeal to
observation that it *is* so. When he looks at the matter in this way,
in the *Appendix*, he abandons the argument about force and
vivacity, and simply says that these different mental states *feel*
different. See pp. 628–9, and especially p. 636. (Oxford Edition.)

belief consists. This he explains by asserting that the original impression communicates some of its force and liveliness to the associated idea, so that the idea is conceived with sufficient vivacity to give rise to belief. This view, he thinks, is confirmed by the fact that when there arises in my mind not an impression, but only the idea of the cause, while my mind still passes to the idea of the effect, this idea does not carry with it a belief in the existence of the effect.

Hume now remarks, that his 'beating about the neighbouring fields' has yielded some result, since in the course of this analysis we have insensibly discovered a new relation between cause and effect, when we least expected it. This relation is their *constant conjunction*; contiguity and priority in time of the cause over the effect, the relations which we previously discovered, are not of themselves sufficient without constant conjunction. But it must be admitted, he goes on, that this relation of constant conjunction helps us very little on our way towards what we are looking for, viz. necessary connexion. From the mere repetition of any past impressions, even to infinity, there will never arise any new idea such as that of necessary connexion: indeed, the number of impressions has in this case no more effect than if we confin'd ourselves to one only.

What then are we to say of this idea of necessary connexion, which seems to be the most important constituent in the relation of cause and effect? Whence does it arise, and of what does it consist? We have seen that it is a new and original idea which is not to be found by analysis of any one instance, and which, while it arises from the repetition of many instances, yet cannot be produced simply by the repetition of instances, in any one of which it is not to be found. The answer must be sought in the fact that this repetition of instances, while it can never produce an impression of a new quality *in the object*, yet can produce an effect *on the mind*, the observation of which effect gives rise to a new impression. For after we have observed a certain number of instances, we feel a determination of the mind necessarily to pass from one object to the other: this determination of the mind we observe, and we thus receive an impression of necessity, which is nothing but a necessity of the mind, determining it to pass from one impression or idea to another. This then is the essence of necessity: it is something that exists in the mind, not in objects; it is not possible for us to form the most distant idea of it considered as a quality of objects. Thus whether we speak of the necessity which makes two times two equal to four, or of the necessity or power in the cause to produce its effect, in either case the necessity which we speak of is only the necessity on the mind to have these ideas and beliefs, when it considers its past impressions. To sum up, Hume's final definition of a cause is this: a cause is 'an object precedent and contiguous to another, and so united with it in the imagination, that the idea of the one determines the mind to form the idea of the other, and the impression of the one to form a more lively idea of the other'.[1]

We can now put before ourselves Hume's theory of thought in its completeness. We have already seen that, according to Hume, when the mind of itself without the stimulus of present external objects passes in its operations from one idea to another, it is commonly constrained by

[1] *Treatise*, I. iii, § 14 (p. 172). Here follows a chapter in which Hume gives a number of 'rules by which to judge of causes and effects'. Ibid., I. iii, § 15 (p. 173).

certain principles of association; this Hume laid down
when examining the operations of the imagination. He
now goes further and claims to have proved that in the
apprehension of causal relations the operations of the
mind are the same in kind. He thus lays it down as a
general rule that *whenever* the mind 'passes from the idea
or impression of one object to the idea or belief of another,
it is not determined by reason, but by certain principles
which associate together the ideas of these objects, and
unite them in the imagination'.[1] These principles, he
reminds us,[2] are neither the infallible nor the sole causes
of a union among ideas; not infallible, since one may fix
his attention for some time on one object without going
further; nor sole, since fancy and imagination may range at
will anywhere from heaven to earth. Yet in spite of this
weakness in these principles and this irregularity in the
imagination, it must be emphatically asserted that in these
principles alone is to be found a full and sufficient explanation of all those operations by which the human mind
arrives at knowledge or belief.

This view, as Hume frankly admits, represents all
reasoning as 'a species of sensation':[3] it attempts to explain
thought by explaining away the distinction between thinking and perceiving. When I am convinced of any principle,
he says, it is only an idea which strikes more strongly upon
me; when I give the preference to one set of arguments
above another, I do nothing but decide from my feeling
concerning the superiority of their influence. In other
words, when I *judge*, it is only an idea which strikes more
strongly upon me: when I *infer*, my inference is simply
my feeling of the superior vivacity of certain ideas over
others. Hume does very little to work out for us the impli-

[1] Ibid., I. iii, § 6 (p. 92).   [2] Ibid.   [3] Ibid., § 8 (p. 103).

cations of his view for Logic:[1] this remained to be done systematically a century later by J. S. Mill. But Hume foresaw that inference must be represented as a passage from particular to particular; and he says, with admirable clearness, that 'general or abstract ideas are nothing but individual ones taken in a certain light, and that, in reflecting on any object, 'tis as impossible to exclude from our thought all particular degrees of quantity and quality as from the real nature of things'.[2]

It need hardly be pointed out that Hume's analysis of experience leaves us no ground for a belief in the existence of a permanent identical *self*, remaining the same through all the changes of experience. It is obvious that his principles do not allow the admission of anything permanent underlying change, whether physical or psychical. All we are aware of is separate and distinct perceptions and ideas; though we further learn by analysis that ideas corresponding to these perceptions behave in certain ways according to certain rules. Nowhere can we find evidence for the existence of any *substratum*, physical or spiritual, necessary to support these perceptions. Strictly speaking, in the science of human nature, we should, recognizing the

---

[1] Apart from a few passing remarks, Hume's only serious contribution to logic is contained in one foot-note. Here he remarks that logic has commonly distinguished three separate acts of the understanding, viz. conception, judgement, and inference; but the truth is that these three acts all, properly understood, resolve themselves into the first: in whatever form or order we survey mental operations, the act of the mind never exceeds a simple conception: belief is never anything but 'a strong and steady conception of any idea, and such as approaches in some measure to an immediate impression'. *Treatise*, I. iii, § 7 (pp. 96–7). Such a view would require a rewriting of all the detail of logic: but this Hume never attempted to do.

[2] Ibid., § 14 (p. 161).

activity of a law of universal attraction, here, as in physics, discipline ourselves always to speak of ideas attracting one another or becoming associated, never of a mind or self affecting or controlling its ideas. This is indeed the great triumph of modern science, that, dispensing with the notion of individual agency, it relies on a reciprocal prin- ciple of action and equal and opposite reaction. Here the science of human nature has now won its spurs, following in the wake of physics.

Paradoxical then as it may appear, the new science of psychology establishes itself in the very act of proving that there is no such thing as a mind or a self at all, thus betraying the fundamental conflict of the rationalist and the sceptic in Hume. In his official doctrine of the nature of the self, the sceptic predominates, though as usual the sceptical conclusion depends upon a confidence in his psychological analysis which it is impossible for us to-day to share. Strictly speaking, he says, we should not speak of a mind or a self at all; the truth is that we have not really any such idea. We are nothing but bundles or collections of different perceptions. The mind is but 'a kind of theatre where several perceptions successively make their appearance'.[1] Moreover, we must not be misled even by the notion of a theatre, since 'we have not the most distant notion of the place where these scenes are represented, or of the materials of which it is composed'.[2] It is true that some metaphysicians claim that they can, by some obscure kind of introspection, find an awareness in themselves of a permanent abiding self, but with these Hume can only agree to differ; he cannot himself find any such idea. Nor, as we have seen, does his analysis of thinking give him cause to believe in the existence of a permanent, active

[1] Ibid., iv, § 6 (p. 253).   [2] Ibid.

ego, necessary to the construction of experience as we
know it. While then it is no doubt a curious fact, which
requires to be explained, that men believe in the existence
of, and even the immortality of, their souls or selves, yet
certainly there is no metaphysical evidence to support
these beliefs. If any one thinks, Hume urges, that these
arguments are dangerous to true religion, he should in
fairness bear in mind that the case is quite as strong
against physical science. Strictly speaking this philosophy
neither makes any addition to the arguments for religion,
nor takes anything from them; it leaves everything as
before. And if it represents religious beliefs as inade-
quately grounded in reason, it puts the sciences in no
better case.

We are now faced with the difficult task of determining
what conclusions Hume drew from his analysis of the
intellectual powers of man. In the histories of philosophy,
he is commonly represented as a sceptic; and it is clear
that as he was finishing the first book of his *Treatise*, this
was his view of himself. There is no choice left, he says,
but between a false reason and none at all. 'For my part, I
know not what ought to be done in the present case. . . .
Where am I, or what? From what causes do I derive my
existence, and to what condition shall I return? . . . What
beings surround me? And on whom have I any influence,
or who have any influence on me?'[1] In particular, what is
to become of the hoped-for science of human nature, which
Hume set out to found? Nowhere is there any certainty
or security of belief; 'if we believe that fire warms, or
water refreshes, 'tis only because it costs us too much pains
to think otherwise.'[2] It is small comfort to recognize that
all the other sciences and the whole of human knowledge

[1] *Treatise*, I. iv, § 7 (pp. 268–9).   [2] Ibid. (p. 270).

are involved in the same ruin. The fact remains that at the outset of our voyage we are totally shipwrecked.

Yet Hume recognized that the sceptic contradicts himself, since he relies on the arguments on which his scepticism is based. The truth is that he was less a sceptic than he thought. Though his tendency to scepticism prevented his being universally hailed as the father of the school, to the benefit of Hartley, a far less profound thinker, there has been raised upon the doctrines of Hume a systematic philosophy of human nature which still flourishes in our day. Furthermore, Hume himself contributed much in the early stages of building it. He himself teaches that reason only fails us in order that nature herself may step into the breach, dispelling the clouds and curing us 'of this philosophical melancholy and delirium'.[1] Sceptic as he is, Hume finds himself absolutely and necessarily determined 'to live, and talk, and act like other people in the common affairs of life';[2] and he concludes that the guiding principle in human life generally is something other than reason. Philosophy, though preferable to superstitious belief, is, when all is said, nothing but 'a cold and general speculation, and seldom goes so far as to interrupt the course of our natural propensities'.[3]

The true object of inquiry then is simply to learn from experience how the human mind does in fact behave. If we turn aside firmly from all hypotheses which are 'embraced merely for being specious and agreeable',[4] we may yet hope 'to establish a system or set of opinions, which not true (for that perhaps is too much to be hoped for) might at least be satisfactory to the human mind, and might stand the test of the most critical examination'.[5]

[1] Ibid. (p. 269).   [2] Ibid.   [3] Ibid. (p. 272).
[4] Ibid.   [5] Ibid.

The most important contribution of Hume himself in this field, apart from his moral theory, is his brilliant work concerning the natural history of religion.[1] But there have also been found many philosophers to follow Hume in this hope. These, taking the line of advance which he thus suggested to them, have built a systematic theory of all knowledge and all reality upon the empirical principles of Hume's psychology, more or less modified, putting forward those principles with less caution and reserve than the master himself, at least sometimes, showed. They have argued, in one form or another, that the demand for certainty in knowledge, though an old dream, is a vain one, and that such belief as an impartial analysis of the human mind shows it to be equipped to entertain is of a quite different order, and quite consistent with Hume's account. Thus in one brilliant modern account of Hume's thought,[2] his sceptical side is hardly referred to, and he is held up before us as the great philosophic champion of modern scientific method.

Yet it is difficult to avoid the conclusion that Hume's teaching is in essence sceptical, and such that any philosophical defender of science must challenge it. In spite of Hume's plea, and in spite of the arguments of many modern thinkers in England and America, it must surely be maintained that nothing but truth itself can really be 'satisfactory to the human mind'; only that which is true can ultimately 'stand the test of the most critical examina-

[1] In his dissertation entitled *The Natural History of Religion*, Hume distinguishes between the rational basis or 'foundation in reason' of religious belief and its 'origin in human nature'. His treatment of the latter problem, considered as a subject apart, marks an important step forward in the development of the scientific study of the nature of the mind.

[2] *Hume*, by T. H. Huxley.

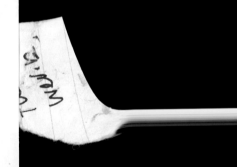

tion'.[1] It was a true instinct which led Hume to see that his theory of knowledge would not consort with any positive teaching whatsoever. Moreover, with unerring judgement, Hume himself touches the spot, and displays the central point of his whole system. 'There are two principles', he says, 'which I cannot render consistent, nor is it in my power to renounce either of them; viz. that all our distinct perceptions are distinct existences, and that the mind never perceives any real connexion among distinct existences'.[2] Real connexion cannot be apprehended by perception; are we then to say it cannot be apprehended at all? Or is it apprehended in some other way? Here Hume confesses himself beaten; he has indeed represented our experience as wholly explicable without supposing that we can apprehend real connexion at all; yet in the last resort he is not quite satisfied that we do not perhaps apprehend it. 'For my part', he says, 'I must plead the privilege of a sceptic, and confess that this difficulty is too hard for my understanding; I pretend not, however, to pronounce it absolutely insuperable'.[3] It is rather in this light, as challenging others to 'wake from their dogmatic slumber'[4] and solve a problem—too difficult indeed for Hume himself, but such that until a solution of it is found philosophic inquiry must remain bankrupt and resourceless—that Hume is most properly regarded.

3. Moral Theory.

As we should expect, Hume maintains that moral distinctions are not derived from reason. Morals, he says, excite

---

[1] *Treatise*, I. iv. § 7 (p. 272).
[2] Ibid. Appendix (p. 636).   [3] Ibid.
[4] Kant says that it was the work of Hume which 'waked me from my dogmatic slumber'.

passions, and produce or prevent actions. Reason of itself is utterly impotent in this particular. Reason, strictly speaking, can have an influence on our conduct only in two ways: 'either when it excites a passion by informing us of the existence of something which is a proper object of it; or when it discovers the connexion of causes and effects, so as to afford us means of exerting any passion'.[1] These are the only kinds of judgement which can in any sense be said to produce actions. These judgements are of course liable to error, and so are sometimes said, though in a figurative and strictly improper way of speaking, to render the actions unreasonable. But it is to be noticed that such errors of judgement are so far from being the source of all immorality, that, being nothing more than mistakes of fact, they are treated with sympathy rather than blame even by the most austere moralists. Properly speaking, no action is reasonable or unreasonable. 'Reason is, and ought only to be, the slave of the passions, and can never pretend to any other office than to serve and obey them'.[2]

In these arguments, according to Kant, Hume is simply asserting, frankly and uncompromisingly, what all previous moral theories had implied. All moral philosophers since Aristotle had in the end allowed that reason itself, pure and unaided, could not move to action; and this is really to admit that in the practical life reason is the slave of 'external springs of action'. If this is so, the importance of Hume is that he is seeking to determine what moral theory is compatible with a fundamental axiom which is universally admitted. Kant's view is that no moral theory is compatible with this principle; that is to say, that to admit this principle is to be a moral sceptic. Moreover, he considers that Hume's moral theory has finally proved

[1] *Treatise*, III. i, § 1, (p. 459).   [2] Ibid. II. iii, § 3 (p. 415).

this, and thus has rendered philosophy the service of demonstrating why all previous moral theories have failed.

But this is not Hume's view. He shows great impatience with moral sceptics; and, for himself, he experiences little difficulty in giving what he regards as a perfectly adequate account of moral experience compatibly with the principle that reason is the slave of the passions. All we have to do, he thinks, is to recognize that the moral principles which guide our actions are not based on reason, but arise rather from natural dispositions of the mind due to experience, and to observe action closely in order to discover scientifically what these principles are, how they come into being, and how they operate. Praise and blame, pride and remorse, he says, are sentiments, not judgements; they are feelings of pleasure and pain. Take any action which is considered vicious, say wilful murder. If you observe it simply as a matter of fact, you will find only certain passions, motives, volitions, and thoughts—there is no other matter of fact in the case. The vice entirely escapes you so long as you consider only the object. You will not find the vice, until you turn your attention to the sentiment of disapprobation in your own breast towards the action. This disapprobation, no doubt, is a fact; but ''tis the object of feeling, not of reason; it lies in yourself, not in the object'.[1] Thus vice and virtue may be compared to sounds, colours, heat and cold, and to the relation of cause and effect, all of which we have discovered to be, not qualities in the object, but perceptions in the mind.[2]

It may be objected that on this principle all actions which give rise in us to any feeling of pleasure are virtuous, and that all actions which give rise to any feeling of pain are vicious. Hume often writes in the *Treatise* as if he

[1] Ibid., III. i, § 1 (p. 469).   [2] Ibid.

accepted this view, simply arguing that it is because of the presence in us of a strong sense of *sympathy* with our fellow men that the pursuit of pleasure and the avoidance of pain lead us on the whole to abide by principles of conduct which might not at first sight appear consistent with pure hedonism. But in the *Inquiry* there is at least a difference of emphasis, due apparently to Hume's recognition that his earlier view fails to give an adequate account of the virtue of justice. Justice, he explains, provides special difficulties for the view that morality is based on the pursuit of pleasure. No doubt it is a good general rule that 'honesty is the best policy'; but it is a rule which seems to be liable to many exceptions, and, as Hume points out, a sensible knave may well think he will derive most pleasure if, while observing the general rule, he takes advantage of the exceptions.

In view of these considerations, Hume recognizes in the *Inquiry* that more attention must be paid to the universality of the moral law, and to the fact that the moral life cannot be represented purely and simply as a life of pleasure, since we are constantly in practice faced with difficult and unpleasant duties, which have to be done 'on principle'. He therefore abandons a purely hedonistic point of view, and lays stress on the doctrine, which he had mentioned in passing in the *Treatise*, that the pleasures which determine moral conduct are recognizably *different in kind* from other pleasures.[1] Not every sentiment of pleasure and pain, he says, which arises from the consideration of characters and actions, is of that peculiar kind, which makes us praise or condemn. The good qualities of an enemy are hurtful to us, but may still command our respect. It is only when we consider an action

[1] See *Inquiry*, §§ 174-5 (pp. 215-17).

in general, without taking account of the effect of that action upon ourselves, that there arises in us that particular feeling of pleasure or pain, which makes us praise or condemn. No doubt in these cases our personal feelings tend to become confused with specifically moral feelings, but, says Hume, since the feelings are quite distinguishable, a man of temper and judgement may preserve himself from such confusions, and give praise to what deserves it—and also, it is implied, live the life of virtue by doing actions such as those which on these principles he praises.

But, it may be asked, can it fairly be assumed that these specifically moral pleasures are strong enough and influential enough to move the mind to act in the face of the great appetites and passions? Surely the voice of morality is represented here as a 'still small voice' indeed, which could have little or no effect on action, except in those rare cases where the great passions are evenly balanced. Hume recognizes this difficulty; and his answer is that the pleasures connected with the moral judgement are in practice always supported by the sentiment of 'humanity', a sentiment which, as it were, grows by what it feeds on and becomes ever stronger and stronger in the human breast. When a man denominates another man his *enemy* or *rival*, he is understood to speak the language of self-love, and to express sentiments peculiar to himself; but when he bestows on anybody the epithets of *vicious* or *odious* or *depraved*, he then speaks another language, and expresses sentiments in which he expects his audience to concur with him. Here he can 'move some universal principle of the human frame, and touch a string to which all mankind have an accord and symphony'.[1] One man's ambition is not another man's ambition, nor will the same

[1] Ibid., § 222 (p. 272).

event or object satisfy both; but 'the humanity of one man is the humanity of every one, and the same object touches this passion in all human creatures'.[1]

Now the fact that a passion is shared by all men will make the influence of that passion greater in every man. From instances of popular tumults and panics, Hume says, we may learn the influence of society in exciting and supporting any passion which is shared with a multitude; he must be 'more or less than a man, who kindles not in the common blaze'.[2] What wonder then that moral sentiments are found to be of such influence in life, even though they spring from principles which may appear at first sight somewhat small and delicate. For these principles are social and universal; they form in a manner, as Hume puts it, 'the *party* of humankind against vice and disorder'.[3] They unite all the members of society in one desire for and pursuit of the good of their kind, that is, the good of society as a whole. This in a word is the whole truth of morality: that action is good which promotes the happiness of society; and it is the sentiment of humanity which secures that man shall not fail to pursue this end. While the human heart is compounded of the same elements as at present it will never be indifferent to the public good.

This view of moral duty, namely, that it enjoins those actions which are for the good of society as a whole, is confirmed, Hume thinks, by the fact that it is conformable to current theories of practical virtue. Viewed in this way, the life of morality not only is shown to be possible but appears to us with all its most engaging charms. We are not enjoined to useless austerities and rigours, suffering and self-denial. 'Celibacy, fasting, penance,' he says,

[1] *Inquiry*, § 222 (p. 272.)   [2] Ibid., § 224 (p. 275).   [3] Ibid.

'mortification, self-denial, humility, silence, solitude, and the whole train of monkish virtues . . . we learn to transfer to the opposite column and place them in the catalogue of vices'. In place of these nothing appears but 'gentleness, humanity, affability, beneficence, and, even, at proper intervals, play, frolic and gaiety'.[1] We are shown that the whole purpose of virtue is 'to make her votaries and all mankind, during every instant of their existence, if possible, cheerful and happy: nor does she ever part with any pleasure but in hopes of ample compensation in some other period of their lives'.[2] We can perhaps hardly agree with Hume that his principle necessarily carries with it a belief in his somewhat mellow view of virtue as against the doctrines of austerer moralists. But it does, if adopted, deal the death-blow to any view which advocates austerity or asceticism for their own sakes, or enjoins them upon us because they are sanctioned by some mysterious consideration which it is beyond the powers of human understanding to apprehend; and no doubt it has usually been through one or other of these means that an austere morality has, when it has, maintained its hold on mankind at large.

Thus it may fairly be said that Hume is a Utilitarian. It is certainly from Hume that the Utilitarian philosophy of Bentham is, through Helvetius and Beccaria, ultimately derived.[3] The fact that we hear less of Hume, as a forerunner of this philosophy, than of Hartley and Priestley is no doubt due primarily to the fact that there is in Hume's teaching a too definitely sceptical flavour for him to be altogether suitable as the father of a progressive school. But for all that, Hume can be seen to be the giant influence

[1] Ibid., § 219 (p. 270).   [2] Ibid., § 228 (p. 279).
[3] Cf. Halévy, *Growth of Philosophic Radicalism*, pp. 9-13, 42-44

which dominates their thought and development. It is true that Bentham, the master of this school, bases his doctrine on a straightforward calculus of pleasures and pains, which Hume, at least in the *Inquiry*, does not accept as the true principle of morality. But when later on proper psychological support was felt to be wanting in the Benthamite doctrine, and first James Mill and then his son, J. S. Mill, were called upon to supply the deficiency, they gave an account of the origin in the human breast of the moral instinct which can be easily seen to be nothing more than Hume's own account, further refined in detail by a use of the machinery of the association of ideas, also taken from Hume.

The strength of Hume's moral theory is that it gives an at least plausible account of the moral life as it is actually lived; it does not fall into the error of describing virtue as a mode of life which is never, and could never be, attained on this earth. The moral sentiment as defined by him is a real sentiment, recognizable as really existent in the human breast and really operating to move us to action. The weakness of his view lies, as he himself saw, in the account it gives of obligation and of the part played by universal principles in the moral life. There is no place in Hume's philosophy for any principle or law which is truly universal. So to any one who feels, as Kant felt, that moral obligation is essentially obligation to obey a universal law for the sake of the law, his teaching must appear as sheer moral scepticism. But to Hume it did not appear so. Any notion of duty for duty's sake seemed to him unworthy of an intelligent being; to tell the truth, for instance, for truth's own sake, quite irrespectively of the known or probable effect of the action on the happiness of society at large, an action which to Kant was always and without exception an inescapable duty, would have seemed to Hume, both in his practical life and in his moral theory, the merest foolishness. The aim of such maxims is to promote the happiness of society; where they defeat their own end, no intelligent man can still feel obliged to obey them. So thought Hume; and, in spite of Kant, there will always be found many to follow him.

4. *Political and Economic Theory.*

While Hume was writing, political philosophy was being profoundly influenced by the works of Montesquieu and Rousseau. Yet it is hardly an exaggeration to say that his own teaching was as important in regard to the subsequent development of political theory and practice in England as were theirs in France and America. His views on political and economic matters were closely connected with his moral and psychological doctrines. Owing to his lifelong interest in the development of the science of human nature, he was never tempted to forget that political and economic institutions are human institutions, and in examining and criticizing them he sought his material directly in the root facts of human nature. To this is due at once his own remarkable acuteness and practical insight in these matters, and also the fact that his writing contains more than the germ of the development of English political thought for at least a century after him.

In working out his own view that all political problems must be solved by the principle of utility, Hume criticized once and for all the theory of a social contract:[1] in this criticism he is followed almost verbally by Adam Smith, Paley, and Bentham. In a limited sense, he maintained, the theory may be accepted. Since men are so nearly

[1] See *Treatise*, III. ii, § 2 (pp. 542 seq.).

equal in physical and mental capacity, the government of
the many by the few must evidently rest upon consent. In
order to protect their external goods, the product of their
labour and good fortune, from the violence of others, men
have inevitably had recourse to a convention, from the
acceptance of which have arisen the ideas of justice and
injustice, of property, right, and obligation. There was
no need for an express promise; a general feeling of common interest sufficed. The invention of organized society
is, like that of language, so simple, and impresses itself so
strongly on the mind, that it is impossible to think that
men can have lived for any length of time without it; we
can only think of man even at his most primitive as living
in a social community. It is legitimate, however, for philosophers to speak of a primitive state of nature in which
society had not yet come into being, provided it is recognized that such a story is no more than a convenient
method of logically expounding the ultimate basis of
political authority. But when the theorists of the social
contract go further than this, as they do, in insisting on
the real existence of a contract, their argument is clearly
inadmissible. In the first place history speaks against
them, since it knows of no such contracts. If this theory
were sound, all existing governments would be illegitimate,
including the English government resting upon the settle-
ment of 1688. In the second place, the theory, considered
simply as a theory, explains nothing and is unnecessary.
By it the duty of obeying the government is based on the
obligation to keep a promise. But on what does this obligation rest? The truth is, says Hume, that both obligations
alike rest on considerations of utility. The duty to keep
a promise does not explain political obligation, but itself
rests on the fact that without it organized society is not

possible, and that without this in turn the happiness of mankind evidently cannot be secured.

It is clear throughout his writings that the application by Hume of the principle of utility to political and economic problems results in doctrines of a decidedly conservative flavour. It is not difficult to foreshadow the arguments of his followers, Burke and Bentham, who based themselves on this principle in taking their stand against the doctrines underlying the French Revolution.[1] This conservatism can be detected at once in Hume's account of property. He repudiates Locke's attempt to base the right of property on labour, and founds it rather on the effect of habit and on established associations—occupation, prescription, accession, and succession. Men have never tried to arrange it on a basis of labour, or even directly on utility, since the difficulties of distribution on these principles are insuperable. So great have been the effect on their minds of these other associations of ideas, that when they have guaranteed the right of property they have done so on this basis: any other arrangement would defeat the end it was meant to serve, namely the happiness of mankind.

In general Hume admits that he inclines to the side of those who would bind tighter the bonds of authority. *Fiat iustitia ruat caelum* is manifestly false; it sacrifices human happiness, which is the end, to the means. *Salus populi suprema lex* is the true maxim; and no doubt it sometimes justifies recourse to insurrection. The question is to know how much necessity is required to justify it; this is a difficult matter and Hume admitted that he wished to range himself with those who incline to insist on obedience. It may seem strange at first sight that he, the sworn enemy

[1] Cf. Halévy, *Growth of Philosophic Radicalism*, p. 140.

of prejudice, should favour a conservatism which is admittedly based on a prejudice.[1] But the explanation is not really far to seek. Hume thought that *all* human beliefs are prejudices, and further that the safest thing in the conduct of life is to follow, not reason, but practical instinct. What he detested was not prejudice, but prejudice setting itself up as truth. He would have admitted that his own belief in the importance of security in the interests of human happiness was based on an association of ideas; but he demanded a like admission from others.

In approaching his views on economics, it must be remembered that 'political economy grew out of political philosophy, and that Hume is still in the transition stage'.[2] He believes in the possibility of a science of economics, though he does not use the term. His interest here as elsewhere is chiefly concerned in relating phenomena to their roots in human nature; while his view that in all action man pursues his own happiness enabled him easily to take up the simplified attitude necessary to the scientific study of economic life. He admits indeed that the maxim may be false *in fact*; but he insists that it is true for the purposes of politics; and this is all that is necessary.

'Everything in the world', he maintains, 'is purchased by labour, and our passions are the only causes of labour.'[3] Hence all desires and passions, and even avarice and luxury, become spurs to industry. Hume does not indeed agree with Mandeville that 'private vices are public benefits'; he maintains that vice in itself is never of advantage to the community; but he argues that two opposite vices may be

[1] Cf. Halévy, *Growth of Philosophic Radicalism*, p. 140.
[2] Palgrave, *Dictionary of Political Economy*, II. 341.
[3] Essay *Of Commerce*.

more advantageous than one alone. 'By banishing *vicious luxury*', he says, 'without curing sloth or indifference to others you only diminish industry.'[1] But while he makes utility and not labour the central point of his economic theory, Hume insists strongly on the claims of the labouring classes. Everybody ought to enjoy, as far as possible, the fruits of his labour in a full possession of all the necessaries and many of the conveniences of life. The state will benefit from this, he thinks, through an increase in capacity to bear taxation; and certainly too great differences in wealth are a source of weakness.

It is only possible here to give a hint of the scope of Hume's work in economics. In the *Essay on Money*, the error of those who held that money was more than a commodity is clearly demonstrated, though Hume was not, of course, the first to refute this view. He does, however, seem to have been the first to argue that it is only during the period of acquisition of money and before the rise in prices that the accumulation of the precious metals is advantageous.[2] The essays of the *Balance* and *Jealousy of Trade* have been recognized to contain a clear statement of sound doctrine. There are also to be found in Hume the beginnings of a theory of population; the growth of population is recognized to be closely dependent upon economic conditions and also closely to affect economic welfare. But Hume has perhaps chiefly earned the admiration of posterity in this sphere by the extraordinary acuteness of his remarks on reading Adam Smith's *Wealth of Nations*. He touches a central weakness when he says—'I cannot think that the rent of farms makes any part of the price of the produce, but that the price is determined altogether by

[1] Essay *Of Refinement in the Arts*.
[2] Cf. Palgrave, *Dictionary of Political Economy*, II. 341.

the quantity and the demand.'[1] This is in accordance with the general sanity of his position; while asserting that everything in the world is purchased by labour, he never forgets that 'our passions are the only causes of labour'.

Enough has been said to show that the tendencies which dominated English political thought in the early nineteenth century are all to be found in Hume. The theories—ethical, psychological, and economic—which combined to make the powerful school of Philosophic Radicalism are all expounded in principle in his pages; it may perhaps even be said that it is there that they meet with their sanest discussion. It is this sanity indeed which is responsible for his receiving less than his due. For it is clear that his temper was too cautious, and his pronouncements too careful and qualified, for him to be hailed with enthusiasm as the father of a progressive school of reform. But so long as it continues to be recognized by philosophers that the fundamental principles of this school are best met by meeting the theories of Hume, it cannot be said that he has altogether failed to receive his due credit.

[1] Rae, *Life of Adam Smith*, p. 286.

CONCLUSION

SOMETHING has already been said of the relations between the Empiricists and the great school of Utilitarians or Philosophical Radicals. The historical relation between the labour theory of value and Locke's view of property is obvious enough. Obvious too is the debt to Hume. Bentham makes full acknowledgement to the treatment of justice in Part III of the *Treatise*. 'I well remember,' he says, 'no sooner had I read that part of the work which touches on this subject than I felt as if the scales had fallen from my eyes.' Hume had there proved once and for all, according to Bentham, by acute argument and by many instances, that the basis of political justice and of morality is utility; 'but I see not,' he added, 'any more than Helvetius saw, what need there was for the exceptions'. Hume's philosophical caution, indeed, and his sense of balance were out of place in the founder of a school of reform. For this reason James Mill, in working out the official psychological doctrines of the school, based his associationist system on the less critical but simpler teaching of Hartley and Priestley. But when it fell to the lot of the younger Mill to write what was in effect a general philosophical justification of English thought, he resorted simply to a more positive and systematic restatement of the teaching of Hume.

It must not be thought, however, that the philosophical influence of the empiricists ended with Mill. The truth is that Locke, Berkeley, Hume, and Mill are in a direct line of development which leads on to the present day; they fit in easily and naturally in the beginnings of that school of thought which seeks to treat the mind, like everything else, as being thrown up as the product of the action and reaction of forces within nature. This school was given a new lease of life by Herbert Spencer's attempt to apply the new categories of development and evolution; yet it is hardly an exaggeration to say, with Dr. Whitehead, that Hume must be given the credit for emphasizing the process inherent in being a mind. No doubt Hume and his predecessors do not lay stress on the time-aspect; but their whole view essentially rests on the representation of complex and sophisticated states of mind, like knowing and believing, as having been developed necessarily and inevitably out of simple experiences, which are taken to be primitive. It is true of course that Locke and Hume actually state their view rather in terms of *composition*, the compounding of simples into complexes—a category which they took from the physics of the day. But their theory can easily be formulated without essential change in terms of development and reaction to environment; the beginnings of this are indeed already to be found in J. S. Mill's treatment of the moral nature of man, though Mill did not foresee the philosophical importance of the new categories. The change of terminology was wholly and self-consciously achieved in Herbert Spencer, with the extreme dogmatism which is often found in thinkers who recognize themselves as pioneers. Since then the school of empirical mental science has gone forward without ever looking back. Most of the work however has been done departmentally; the general principles have been progressively applied to the various special problems presented to mental science, and have been to some extent refined and modified in the course of their application. After Mill no important attempt was made to vindicate the general philosophy of the position, by working out systematically the whole theory of human nature involved in it, until the foundation of the school of pragmatism by William James.

With this latter school we need not directly concern ourselves here: but it will be worth while to give a very brief consideration to the views of Mill, in the attempt to throw some light on the question as to what is living and what is dead in the thought of the empiricists. After Hume, as is well known, there had arisen in Germany, starting with Kant, a great new school of idealism, whose doctrines arose largely out of criticism of the views of the English philosophers. Though the doctrines of this school were hardly known in England, it was the general opinion elsewhere that philosophy had been rendered bankrupt by the writings of Hume, but had taken on a new lease of life with the philosophy of Kant. Now Mill had himself read much of the work of Kant; and he had been profoundly affected at a critical period of his life by Coleridge, who had been more influential than anybody else up to that time in introducing German thought into England. Furthermore one of Mill's most mature works, the *Examination of Sir William Hamilton's Philosophy*, was written in criticism of the view of one whose theory of thinking was essentially Kantian. Thus an examination of the philosophy of Mill, who in spite of these influences remained unconvinced by the Kantian arguments, is especially helpful in the attempt to determine what in the thought of the empiricists survived the criticism of Kant. But as a preliminary it will be necessary to say a few words about Kant himself.

It is not very difficult, in view of modern research, to explain in general terms the Critical position which Kant laid down as the necessary starting-point of all future philosophy, so long as we consider it only as a starting-point. It is very difficult indeed to determine what con-

824146   L

clusions really follow from the adoption of this position, or even to state what conclusions were thought to follow by Kant; but fortunately these points are of little direct concern to us here. Kant starts from the conviction that both rationalists and empiricists have failed; and their failure he puts to himself in this way. The rationalists thought that all knowledge was the product of pure thinking, of which mathematics is the type; that is to say, it is the product of the mind's own activity, the essence of the mind being to think. Thus for them perception played no part in knowledge at all, except to pull a trigger, as it were, and thereby to be the necessary occasion of the mind's being active in its own essential manner, viz. thinking. This view breaks down because of the difficulties connected with innate principles, and also because nobody really believes that perception plays no contributory part in knowledge at all, especially in view of the emphasis laid on observation and experiment by modern science. The empiricists, on the other hand, sought to maintain that all knowledge was through and through grounded in perception: in their hands this came to mean that all knowing is perceiving; and thus either the existence of thought was denied altogether, or else thinking was regarded as making no contribution to knowledge. This view inevitably resulted in the scepticism of Hume.

Having put the situation to himself in this way, Kant inevitably sought to steer a middle way between the two views. In the early days his view is in general not unlike that of Locke: knowledge can be divided into two parts— pure *a priori* knowledge, which is beyond all doubt, and sensitive knowledge, of which we can perhaps make ourselves sceptical if we have the will. Thus he speaks of mathematics as wholly *a priori*, and also of a pure *a priori* physics, small no doubt in area, but not to be denied; he seems to have thought of it as consisting of two or three formal principles which serve as the starting-point for empirical physics. But in the course of time the spectre of Hume prevented him from working out this view. The theory which in his maturer thought he puts forward is an original one of his own. In *all* experience, he seeks to maintain, at any and every moment when the mind is conscious, this consciousness is, as it were, the product or resultant of two forces—a force exerted by the object and a force exerted by the intrinsic activity of the mind. Thus the character of any given concrete experience is determined partly by the character of the object and partly by the character of the mind. The empiricists saw that the particular nature of an actual experience was determined by the characteristics of the object present in perception; but they failed to see that the object could not have exactly the effect it does have on the mind unless the mind were a mind. This important point they missed in their anxiety to vindicate the importance of sense-perception in knowledge. Careful analysis shows, however, according to Kant, that experience as we know it could only have come about in the way described by Locke, Berkeley, and Hume, if there exists, as a precondition of the process they describe, a mind with a certain independent nature of its own.

So far Kant's account seems reasonable; at the very least, his view that experience can only be explained on the presupposition of an active mind is a hypothesis well worth working out. But, as might be expected, Kant's own working out of it has not proved to be altogether unexceptionable. His own view is that it is possible, by a special method of his own, to determine what are the essential characteristics of this spontaneous activity of mind, which is one of the two essential factors in the growth of experience; and thereby also to determine what influence this factor is bound to have in the course of the formation of actual experience, as we know it. He therefore proceeds to work out a *Critique of Pure Reason*, in which he intends, as the name implies, to isolate the contribution to knowledge of pure reason, always remembering—though in practice of course he by no means always remembers—that we have no actual experience of the functioning of pure reason, which is only one determinant ingredient in actual experience and is not capable of being experienced separately. Thus the psychological method of Hume is of no use to Kant, since it proceeds by the analysis of real, concrete experience. He is therefore forced to find a new method, which may be capable of isolating this abstract element in experience. This method he calls the 'transcendental method'. The exact nature of this method, and the question of its success in the hands of Kant and of the Idealists who follow him, does not concern us. It only needs to be said that the importance of the Critical position in philosophy has often been obscured by the fact that the exact task which it led Kant to set himself, a critique of the purely rational element in cognition, often led both Kant and his critics to speak as if he were trying to explain all experience, in all its actual fullness, as wholly generated by pure reason alone. It is quite clear from a careful examination of Kant's work that this is not his considered view: but it is equally clear that all his writing is not consistent with his mature position. This point is only of importance here, in that the hostility of Mill and other subsequent English thinkers to Kant's philosophy has been partly due to this misrepresentation of it. A much more important cause of their hostility, however, is to be found in deeper and simpler considerations, which have little or nothing to do with an understanding of the details either of Kant's method or of the resulting system of philosophy.

There is no doubt that Kant's own view, worked out by the transcendental method, evades Locke's attack on innate principles. Carefully stated, it also perhaps evades much of Hume's criticism of the causal principle, though this is admittedly a difficult matter to determine. But the attitude of Mill and other empirical philosophers seems to be based rather on a positive faith which is essentially and fundamentally hostile to Kant's whole standpoint. Kant comes to terms with the rationalists, where the empiricist feels that they must be destroyed root and branch. No doubt it is true that the apriorism and subjectivism of Kant have been commonly overestimated, and that most attacks on him miss the essentials of the Critical position. But however cautiously his view is stated, the fact remains that Kant thought that the mind has a certain independent, irreducible nature of its own; and that this intrinsic nature ultimately informs all its experience, and especially its knowledge and its beliefs. On his view there are certain features in experience—and he claims to exhibit in some detail what these features are—which can never be wholly explained in terms of experience, but must be admitted to be transcendentally conditioned by the original nature of mind. This the empiricist can never admit.

Mill, basing himself on Berkeley, accepts the general position that all knowledge and all beliefs are nothing but the product of conscious experience; any beliefs which we have have been forced on the mind in the process of conscious experience. Even if there seem to be in the mind convictions of any kind which are so universal as to appear inseparable from the very existence of mind, this must be explained naturalistically:—events in nature, it must be said, have behaved so absolutely regularly and have occurred in such huge numbers that the mind would be bound to believe in their absolute conformity to these principles. Even our certainty with regard to mathematics and our confidence in the principle of the uniformity of nature itself must be explained in this way. No resort to the *a priori*, as a kind of *deus ex machina*, is allowable in theory of knowledge. In this respect the pure categories of Kant are as obnoxious as the innate ideas of the Cartesians; both are bound ultimately to conflict with the spirit and attitude of science. Even Kant at his most cautious allows for the existence of principles which, as regulative of its activity, are universally binding on the mind throughout the interpretation of experience—so that experience is powerless to cause any change or modification in them. No doubt, on Kant's mature view, none of the actual laws as actually formulated and used by any science are of this pure, unchangeable nature; it is only the pure formal principles, which in some sense underlie the development of the laws formulated by the sciences, that are *a priori* and universal. But when all is said, this view represents the mind as in essence unmalleable to its experience, and its knowledge as in the end formally determined, not only in extent but also in its essential nature, by the intrinsic character and capacities of the knowing mind. To this the empiricist has always objected. Unless the categories of the mind are generated in the mind through and through by its conscious experience, then observation and experiment are not the vital things in knowledge, and the case for empiricism fails. This Mill saw, and he resisted the *a priori* as much in the new form as his predecessors had resisted it in the old, and for the same reasons.

Now this is a very strong position; a position, moreover, which has derived further strength from the striking revolutions in the categories of the sciences in the last quarter of a century, and also from the diminished dogmatism of the great scientific writers of recent years. Science seems to be claiming more and more to throw doubt upon and to reformulate even the most fundamental laws of thought. We hear on all sides, for instance, that two straight lines can enclose a space, and that two particles of matter can occupy the same point in space at the same time; similarly in some contemporary logic, it appears, even the law of excluded middle has not remained inviolate. These developments are alleged to be necessary to the possibility of any interpretation of the facts observed. Small wonder is it that *a priori* is to-day hardly a term to conjure with; naturally there are many adherents to the school of thought which seeks to explain the generation and development of categories wholly in terms of experience. Much brilliant research has been accomplished in the various departments of this school; and under its philosophical protection, empirical psychology has gone forward by leaps and bounds. Yet it is doubtful whether any important step has been taken in advancing the general philosophical position implied; though there has certainly grown up an ever-increasing hardihood in putting forward as fundamental matter of faith principles of which Hume was more than a little diffident. Whatever be the ultimate verdict on the Pragmatists, considered as a school of general philosophy—there is no doubt of the brilliance of their contribution to psychology and the social sciences—it is certain that Mill, for all his sympathetic understanding and brilliant exposition, added nothing of importance to the philosophical teaching of Hume; and, whether or not the same may be said in as unqualified a manner of William James, it is certain that his debt to the empiricists was immeasurably great.

It must be remembered, however, that the opposing school of Kant also has had a brilliant career. After all, Kant had driven serious wedges into the empiricist position. At the least he put up a very strong case for his contention that the possibility of a systematic inquiry, like physics or modern biology, can never be explained without the postulate of an active mind. The view of the world as a unity—and both each separate science and each individual mind presents the world to itself as a unity—could never be forced by any experience on an entirely characterless mind. The mind cannot be malleable to its experience in all respects at once; if it were, our experience would be the chaos which Hume saw in his sceptical nightmare. In actual fact, moreover, it can be shown that any given science could have developed as it did only if certain formal categories had been universally binding; for instance, the natural philosopher has in the sphere of physics always assumed without exception the formal principle of conservation. And while in any given case such practical acceptance of principles without criticism may appear as a defect, hindering perfect open-mindedness, it can be shown that, without something of the kind, no systematic inquiry would be possible at all, whether in philosophy or science. Thus Kant did well to give a start to that great series of nineteenth-century works on logic, which sought to investigate in detail this aspect of the mind's activity. The method of these logics is a peculiar one, differing from that of empirical psychology, and having a special and difficult technique of its own. It may be that Kant and some others have been unduly dogmatic about its claim to be the one true method of that architectonic philosophy which is to put the special sciences and their method in a subordinate place. But there is no doubt that the Idealist Logic has offered brilliant contributions to modern theory of knowledge, and has been not without its effect on empirical psychology. Perhaps its chief service has been that by its analysis of the method of empirical science it has drawn attention to the substratum of dogmatism which has been found to lie underneath the Empiricist philosophy itself.

Locke, Berkeley, and Hume are then, in a very real sense, responsible for the emergence both of modern Idealism and of the philosophy of Experience. Kant allowed to Locke the credit of opening the way to the Critical philosophy, while Hume woke him from his dogmatic slumber and forced upon him the Critical position. It is the chief sign of the greatness of these philosophers that the main body of their thought is included within the system of both schools. Hume, in particular, is seen at his greatest in this, that while founding a school of thought whose fruitful inquiry has persisted to the present day, he also finally forced upon the attention of philosophers the points at which that school must be attacked.

BIBLIOGRAPHY

LOCKE

Convenient Editions:

Essay concerning Human Understanding. By A. C. FRASER. 2 vols. Oxford, 1894.

On the Conduct of the Understanding. By T. FOWLER. Oxford. 5th ed., 1901.

Essay concerning Human Understanding (Abridged). By A. SETH PRINGLE-PATTISON. Oxford, 1924.

The Philosophical Works of John Locke. (Bohn's Standard Library.) 2 vols., 1902.

Two Treatises on Civil Government. (Morley's Universal Library.) Routledge. 2nd ed., 1887.

Books on Locke:

S. ALEXANDER. Locke. (Philosophies Ancient and Modern.) 1908.

T. FOWLER. Locke. (English Men of Letters Series.) 1880.

A. C. FRASER. Locke. (Blackwood's Philosophical Classics.) 1890.

J. GIBSON. Locke's Theory of Knowledge and its Historical Relations. Cambridge, 1917.

BERKELEY

Convenient Editions:

The Works of George Berkeley. By A. C. FRASER. 4 vols. Oxford, 1871, revised 1901.

A New Theory of Vision and other Select Philosophical Writings (including the 'Principles of Human Knowledge', and 'Dialogues between Hylas and Philonous'). (Everyman's Library.) 1910.

Selections from Berkeley. Ed. A. C. FRASER. Oxford. 6th ed., 1910.

Books on Berkeley.

A. C. FRASER. Berkeley. (Blackwood's Philosophical Classics.) 1881.

G. A. JOHNSTON. The Developement of Berkeley's Philosophy. Macmillan, 1923.

HUME

Convenient Editions.

Treatise of Human Nature. By L. A. SELBY-BIGGE. Oxford. 2nd ed., 1896.

Hume's Enquiries concerning Human Understanding, and the Principles of Morals. By L. A. SELBY-BIGGE. Oxford. 2nd ed. 1902.

Treatise of Human Nature. 2 vols. (Everyman's Library.) 1911.

Essays, Moral, Political and Literary. Ed. by T. H. GREEN, and T. H. GROSE. 2 vols. Longmans, Green & Co. 1875.

Dialogues concerning Natural Religion. Ed. B. McEWEN. Blackwood & Sons, 1907.

Books on Hume.

T. H. HUXLEY. Hume. (English Men of Letters Series.) 1879.

W. KNIGHT. Hume. (Blackwood's Philosophical Classics.) 1905.

C. W. HENDEL. Studies in the Philosophy of David Hume. Princeton University Press, 1925.

A. E. TAYLOR. David Hume and the Miraculous. Cambridge University Press, 1927.

General Books on Locke, Berkeley, and Hume.

T. H. GREEN. Introductions to Hume's 'Treatise of Human Nature'. Collected Works, vol. i. Longmans, Green & Co., 1890.

A. SETH PRINGLE-PATTISON. Scottish Philosophy. Blackwood & Sons, 1907.

N. K. SMITH. Studies in the Cartesian Philosophy. Macmillan, 1902.

R. ADAMSON. The Development of Modern Philosophy. Blackwood & Sons, 1908.

W. R. SORLEY. History of English Philosophy. Cambridge. 1920.

INDEX